BUILD-A-BARN

NO PATTERN CONSTRUCTION

JULIE SEFTON

American Quilter's Society

PO Box 3290 • Paducah, KY 42002-3290
Fax 270-898-1173 • e-mail: orders@AQSquilt.com

The American Quilter's Society or AQS is dedicated to quilting excellence. AQS promotes the triumphs of today's quilter, while remaining dedicated to the quilting tradition. We believe in the promotion of this art and craft through AQS Publishing and AQS QuiltWeek®.

CONTENT EDITOR: CAITLIN RIDINGS
GRAPHIC DESIGN: ELAINE WILSON
COVER DESIGN: MICHAEL BUCKINGHAM
HOW-TO PHOTOGRAPHY: JULIE SEFTON
BARN PHOTOGRAPHY: JULIE SEFTON, UNLESS OTHERWISE NOTED
QUILT PHOTOGRAPHY: CHARLES R. LYNCH
ASSISTANT EDITOR: ADRIANA FITCH
PRODUCTION MANAGER: SARAH BOZONE
DIRECTOR OF PUBLICATIONS: KIMBERLY HOLLAND TETREV

American Quilter's Society
www.AmericanQuilter.com

Library of Congress Cataloging-in-Publication Data

Names: Sefton, Julie.
Title: Build-a-barn : no pattern construction / by Julie Sefton.
Description: Paducah, KY : American Quilter's Society, [2016]
Identifiers: LCCN 2016006227 (print) | LCCN 2016008749 (ebook) | ISBN
  9781604604115 (pbk.) | ISBN 9781604603361 (e-book)
Subjects: LCSH: Quilting--Patterns. | Barns in art. | Seasons in art.
Classification: LCC TT835 .S4425 2016 (print) | LCC TT835 (ebook) | DDC
  746.46--dc23
LC record available at http://lccn.loc.gov/2016006227

RIGHT: Detail photo of barn near Ann Arbor, Michigan. PHOTO: Lynn Carson Harris

Contents

Barn with hay bales in northern Mississippi PHOTO: Larry Sefton

OPPOSITE: SEE ROCK CITY, detail, full quilt on p. 27

Introduction

West Tennessee barn **PHOTO:** Sammie Ballard

This book is the result of a happy collision between passion and process.

Passion – I have always loved barns, especially the weathered ones that sag, lean, and proudly wear their age. I am fascinated by their textures, layers, shapes, and shadows, and enjoy imagining the stories these aging survivors could tell.

Process – As a quilt maker, I have been inspired by countless patterns but, for a variety of reasons, my quilts rarely end up looking like the project photos. Sometimes my change of direction is a matter of personal preference, but many times my restlessness is caused by boredom. Simply following directions is just not enough. I crave context and I want to be involved from beginning to end. The process of free piecing offers all of that and more.

A fellow blogger put it this way: *"I like unique and free pieced better than 'yikes, they're everywhere' quilts,"* and so do I.

In these pages I have shared the creation story of my free pieced barn quilt SEE ROCK CITY as an in-depth overview of the free piecing process from gestation through construction, layout issues, quilting, and beyond.

Detailed process notes provide step-by-step information to design and create four unique free pieced barn blocks. Additional process notes show how to combine those blocks to make your very own SEASONAL SAMPLER.

The Gallery's extraordinary gathering of sixteen all-new free pieced barn quilts will excite and inspire you as will the stories shared by their international designers/makers. (Visit http://thefreepiecedbarnproject.blogspot.com for more on the Gallery quilts.)

I hope you'll join us in the sometimes challenging, yet, deeply soul-satisfying world of free piecing!

Julie Sefton

Memphis, Tennessee

Prologue

To begin at the very beginning, I need to introduce you to two very special people.

Longarm quilt artist Chris Ballard of Oakland, Tennessee, who blogs at Quilting4U (http://quilting4u.blogspot.com).

Artist Lynne Tyler of Goffstown, New Hampshire, who blogs at The Patchery Menagerie (http://patcherymenagerie.blogspot.com). Lynne also posts on her cat's blog at Darling Millie (http://darlingmillie.blogspot.com).

Chris and I met, by chance, in 2004 at a local quilt shop. She was just starting to quilt for others and I was a new quiltmaker in need of a quilter. Since that day, we have become good friends and continue to challenge each other artistically—finishing well over 200 quilts together.

Lynne and I discovered each other and our blogs during Tonya Ricucci's international online free pieced gathering The Lazy Gal Summer Quilting Class of 2008.

When I learned that Lynne made custom kitty quilts, I ordered three (one for our cat and two for my mother-in-law's furry companions).

Chris (L) and Lynne (R) with Lynne's ready-for-quilting BRIGHT CRAYONS quilt top.

Julie (L) with Angel (her cat) and Chris (R) holding Lynne's newly quilted sampler quilt, LETTERS FROM HOME. **PHOTO:** Larry Sefton

Julie (L) and Lynne (R) with Millie (the traveling cat) at the start of their October 2013 St. Louis road trip. **PHOTO:** Larry Sefton

Free Piecing – My Definition
Open-ended, original, and personal.
Joyfully dependent upon individual
    interpretation.
Deliberate yet spontaneous.
Sometimes whimsical.
Sometimes serious.
Always engaging.

Those early email exchanges and our shared love of liberated, free pieced quilts formed the basis of what is now an amazing long-distance friendship.

In late 2008 when Lynne needed a longarm quilter for her free pieced sampler quilt, LETTERS FROM HOME, I suggested she contact Chris. Now, when Lynne is asked why she ships each of her quilts over 1,200 miles to be quilted, she just smiles and says, "Stop and really look at my quilts —you'll understand."

In 2010 the international free piecing community celebrated the release of Word Play Quilts by Tonya Ricucci. Lynne and I had three quilts included in that book, and Chris quilted all three.

In late 2011 Lynne shared the making of her free pieced class sample THE FOUR SEASONS on her blog. She also mentioned that she might host a four season quilt-along. In a blinding "light bulb moment" I knew what I needed to do. Instead of making a four season sampler with free pieced houses, I finally had the perfect setting for my long-loved and much-thought-about barns! However, life intervened and Lynne's quilt-along did not happen, but my plan for making free pieced barns persisted.

"I still want to do this except I don't want to make houses," I told Lynne. "I want to make barns."

"So make barns." she told me. "They're not that different. It's the same basic construction."

THE FOUR SEASONS, 48" x 60", Designed and pieced by Lynne Tyler, Goffstown, New Hampshire. Quilted by Chris Ballard, Oakland, Tennessee.

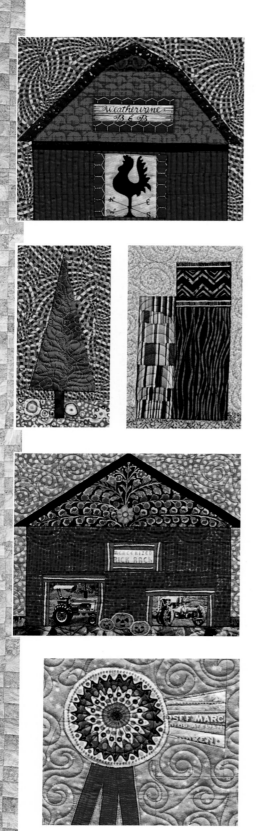

A few of SEE ROCK CITY's details, full quilt on p. 29

"I don't want to do the four seasons the same way you did. I want mine to be different. I was thinking of making a barn for each month."

"That's a good idea, but if you're going to do barns in Tennessee where it doesn't snow, you have to find a way to let your viewers know which month of the year it is. What does the ground look like in March? What does the sky look like? What's different about July? November?" Lynne then suggested I draw my barns out first so I could figure out how to piece them together before I started sewing.

"I can't draw."

"You don't have to make it look real, you just need an outline of where things are going to go."

As I shared my work in progress, Lynne continued to offer this same kind of no-nonsense moral support and honest feedback. When it was time for SEE ROCK CITY to be longarm quilted, Chris spent hours adding textures and details. Her custom free motion artistry truly transformed SEE ROCK CITY from flimsy to fabulous.

Through all of this, the three of us formed lasting friendships. We have shared thousands of emails and untold hours of telephone conversations about creativity, parenting, cats, dogs, day jobs, families, process, collaboration, and—most importantly for the sake of this book—the joys and challenges involved in making free pieced quilts.

Who could ever have imagined that a series of chance encounters would lead to the ongoing adventures we continue to share.

Here's to the magic of serendipity!

LEFT TO RIGHT: Lynne, Julie, and Chris holding their collaborative quilt MAGIC HAPPENS.
PHOTO: Lynne Tyler

The Free Pieced Barn Project

Barn near Ann Arbor, Michigan
PHOTO: Lynn Carson Harris

By the end of 2011 my design wall held twelve groupings of fabrics arranged so the various sky and ground colors moved through the west Tennessee seasons. Colors and textures were chosen to suit the "look" of each month and lend compositional balance to the three barns wide by four barns high "postcards on a scrapbook page" layout I saw in my mind.

The Colors

As I auditioned fabrics for my barns, I knew I wanted each barn to be unique. I also knew I wanted one barn to be a completely different color.

Sorting and considering fabrics for each month's block

Preserved historic farm building near Memphis, Tennessee

Distressed barn building near Memphis, Tennessee (built 1949 – demolished 2014)

But why did I instinctively choose so many reds?

Until the late 1700s most barns were not painted—the right wood used in the right location did not need the protection of paint. As time passed, barn builders began using more and more unseasoned wood and constructing buildings without as much consideration for their exposure to sun, water, and wind. Enter the need for paint.

Early paints were a mixture of linseed oil and milk resulting in a whitewash effect. The wood was coated and the white stayed in place for quite a while, but the wood was not well protected from decay.

Through trial and error, barn owners discovered a mixture of linseed oil, turpentine, and rust scrapings did a better job of preventing mold. The rust scrapings were later replaced with iron oxide-rich soil since dirt was more plentiful and less expensive than hard to get pigments for colors like green or yellow. Depending on the particular blend of oil, turpentine, and soil, colors ranged from darkish oranges through all shades of red and on into browns.

Even with today's wide array of standardized colors, familiar shades of red remain near the top of the list.

Advertising on Barns?

All along, I knew that I wanted to include signage on my barns. However, not all barns have signs. For those who are not familiar with the concept of outdoor advertisements painted on roadside barns, here is a quick overview:

In the 1890s the Bloch Brothers started advertising their tobacco products on the sides of barns. Best known for their Mail Pouch barns, by the 1960s they had painted advertising on barns along highways in 22 states. Folk hero Harley E. Warrick (1924-2000) is credited with painting most of those 20,000 barns.

Other products such as competing brands of tobacco, liquor, motor oils, tourist attractions like Ruby Falls, Meremac Caverns, and Rock City, as well as pharmacy and even food items, were also featured on the sides of barns. The more Americans took to the highways, the more advertising they were likely to see.

In 1965 Congress passed the Highway Beautification Act which dramatically changed the regulation of billboards and advertising near federally-funded highways. As the rules changed, Mail Pouch and other advertising barns decreased in numbers. An Amendment to the Act was passed in 1974 to create "Folk Heritage Barn" status, and the National Barn Preservation Act of 2001 now protects barns 50 years or older from demolition, but despite these efforts, advertising barns are now far less common and are often in very sad condition.

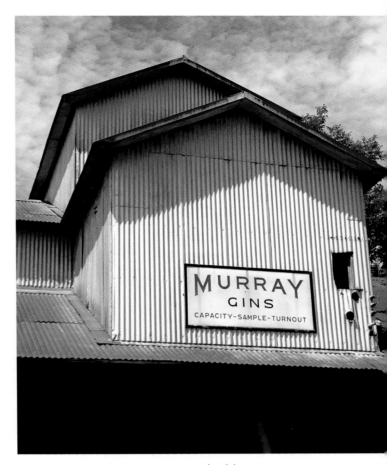

Signage on an empty cotton gin building near Arlington, Tennessee

January's barn, signage detail

February's barn, signage detail

May's barn, signage detail

March's barn, signage detail

The Layout–
Version One

Rock City is located at the top of Lookout Mountain, Georgia, near Chattanooga, Tennessee. This sign is located near Lover's Leap (visible along the right side of the photo).

Photos taken during author's visit to Rock City

believe that every quilt needs its own name and the best names invite viewers into the quilt's story. I named my free pieced barn quilt to honor a much-loved piece of Americana – the Rock City barns.

Transcribed from sign shown at left: "Since Rock City was off the beaten path, Garnet Carter had to devise a way to get the public up the mountain to see this unique attraction. In 1936 he dreamed up a new kind of road sign, one that ultimately became as famous as Rock City itself. Summoning a young painter named Clark Byers, he told him of his plan to paint an advertising message on the roof of barns along major highways. By the 1950s, Garnet's message was painted on over 800 barns from Michigan to Texas to Florida. Journalists began calling Clark and his helpers the 'Barnyard Rembrandts,' and vacationers by the thousands heeded the call to 'See Rock City'."

Garnet and his wife Frieda opened Rock City to the public in 1932. While Garnet was busy with other entrepreneurial projects, Frieda had invested her time and energy into their property's nearly 2-million year old rock formations, with the goal of creating a gigantic rock garden. (Her earliest paths were literally marked with string.) Later, under Frieda's direction, wildflowers and many other plants were added to the improved trails, along with many of her beloved gnomes and elves imported from her native Germany.

As detailed in the sign, opposite page, Rock City advertising on barns proliferated across a large number of states and the phrase SEE ROCK CITY (or one of its many variations) became a familiar sight for travelers.

In the 1960s Byers was forced to paint over any unlicensed Rock City barns under the terms of Lady Bird Johnson's *Beautify America* campaign, leaving less than half of the 800 barns intact.

Byers tried to keep the attraction's marketing concept alive by building red mail boxes bearing the Rock City slogan but the U.S. Postal Service did not approve. Byers then turned his mail box concept into birdhouses, one of the attraction's most enduring symbols.

In 1994 photographer David Jenkins drove over 35,000 miles through 14 states to document nearly 255 Rock City barns. Sadly, many of those 255 barns have now fallen down, been demolished, or simply faded away.

The massive rock formations of Rock City and the attraction's 14 acres are listed in the book *1,000 Places to See Before You Die*, edited by Patricia Shultz. Rock City has also been named as one of "America's Iconic Places" by National Geographic.

And, as of September 2014, I can honestly say that I have seen Rock City.

RIGHT: Photos taken during author's visit to Rock City

All twelve newly-bordered blocks on design wall in a
4-3-3-2 row arrangement

Numerous blog posts were shared during the construction of SEE ROCK CITY'S twelve free pieced barns. Then, in keeping with my original vision of postcards on a page, I cut 1-inch strips of royal blue to border each of the twelve blocks. Once in place those hard dark edges made me very nervous-what kind of layout would reconcile the wide variety of block sizes?

Determined to trust the process, I started cutting and adding strips of blue Roman Glass background fabric to the design wall mix.

To line up the blocks' horizontal and vertical centers, I devised a system using lengths of thread and painters tape. When I positioned the newly framed blocks using that grid, my heart sank. What I saw was nothing like what I had envisioned.

Blocks on design wall in a 3-3-3-3 layout with test
strips of background fabric

SEE ROCK CITY, version 1 measuring 80" x 90"

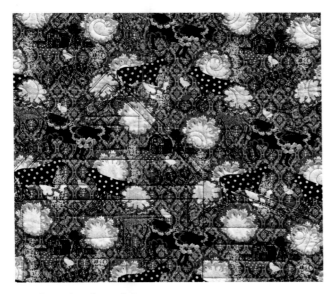

"Perfect" backing fabric

Despite my disappointment, I was determined to turn the barns into a quilt top. Additional adjustments were made until the twelve framed blocks were finally assembled into what I call a "flimsy." I shared this photo (shown above) with my blog readers on April 24, 2012. After so many positive responses to the individual barn blocks, I was unprepared for the overwhelming neutral reactions to the finished quilt top.

Despite that stillness, I pushed forward and began to create a back for my quilt.

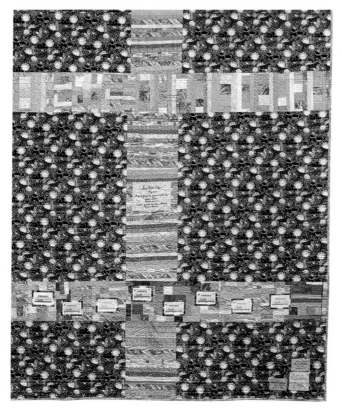

Back of SEE ROCK CITY showing pieced strata

SEE ROCK CITY handwritten label

"Perfect" backing fabric had been purchased early in the process, but since the top was now so much larger than anticipated, my yardage was no longer enough. Two rows of 9" wide scrappy strata were pieced together and inserted across the backing's full width, creating five horizontal sections. A 12" wide strip of scrappy strata, including handwritten label, was stitched into the back's full length vertical seam. Little did I know when I created that label it would be another ten months before SEE ROCK CITY would be finished.

Normally when I hand off a project for long arm quilting, I am excited to move forward—but after transferring custody of SEE ROCK CITY to Chris, there was nothing but doubt. Two weeks later, after seeing the photo of SEE ROCK CITY's layout, Lynne's mother, Jeanne Lachance, uttered one word—"Meh" (defined by Dictionary.com as unimpressive or boring). Her response crystallized my nagging doubts and spurred me to action. Within 48 hours I had called Chris and happily retrieved my flimsy.

The Evolution of a Re-imagined Quilt Top

"What a glorious mess is about to happen . . ."

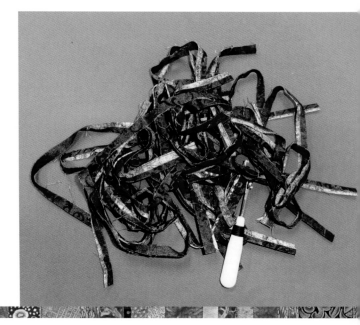

Removing frames from each block

Phase II of my free pieced barn project was formally announced in a blog post on Tuesday, May 23, 2012.

To the astonishment of many, I used my rotary cutter to slice the quilt top (see photo, p. 17) into twelve large sections.

Liberating the individual blocks from that awkward sea of blue background fabric felt amazing!

I began the careful process of unstitching each royal blue border and, as the strips fell away, I felt my spirits lift.

As I worked, I kept thinking about WHY the first layout had failed so spectacularly. Beyond the obvious spatial issues, what was it that bothered me?

Adjectives like stagnant, strait-laced, and stuffy quickly rose to the top of my list.

But how to change that?

When I am deeply puzzled or stumped, I reach for my favorite touchstone books. (See Additional Resources and Suggested Reading List at http://thefreepiecedbarnproject.blogspot.com)

While re-reading *Quilting Lessons, Notes from the Scrap Bag of a Writer and Quilter* by Janet Catherine Berlo, I chanced across this passage: *"It requires seeing connections that are not obvious at first glance. It requires not only long hours of play, but of vision and re-vision. The result? A unique and meaningful whole, not boxed in but set free."*

". . . NOT BOXED IN BUT SET FREE."

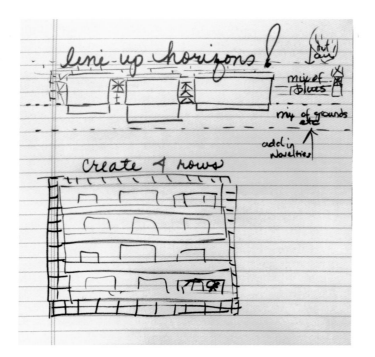

The idea that changed everything.

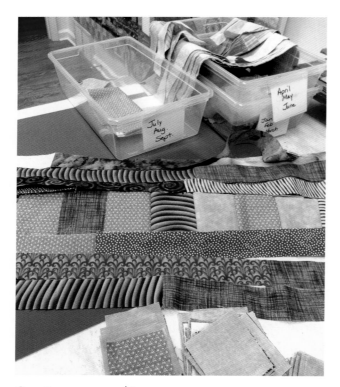

Creating scrappy skies

I had my answer!

In one swift "EUREKA" moment, the earlier nonsense involving horizontal and vertical block centers evaporated.

The answer to my layout issue was clear and simple: LINE UP THE HORIZONS.

That thought quickly led to this one: ". . . and it needs to be far less rigid and much more liberated."

In a flash, I knew what I wanted to achieve AND I knew how to get there.

Quickly I pulled every remaining scrap of the various ground fabrics from my stash, along with a few others that suited each block's monthly mood. I cut randomly sized pieces, loosely sorted them into four seasonal groups, and set them aside.

I rummaged about in my stash for scraps that included a kite and a small red bird. I also ordered several novelty fabrics featuring cows, chickens, sheep, rock layers, hot air balloons, and hay bales.

I gathered whatever remained of the fabrics used in the 12 different skies. Fueled by new energy, I sorted those fabrics into groups—one for each of the quilt's four seasonal rows.

I joyfully cut each group of fabrics into three and four inch strips. Odd shaped pieces were trimmed into rectangles and squares.

One group at a time, I feverishly stitched the strips and pieces into scrappy made-fabric. When I was finished, I had four panels measuring roughly 36" x 40" each.

In early June, I shared photos on my blog.

I was still unstitching royal blue borders when I remembered two long strips of soft-blue four-patches left over from a previous project.

While retrieving the four-patches, I also gathered up the remaining strata segments from SEE ROCK CITY's back.

I pinned these random pieces on one side of the design wall, not sure how or whether to incorporate them into the new layout.

Later, when I glanced at the design wall, there was no question.

I quickly cut narrow strips for an inner border. The four-patch and strata sections were arranged around the soft brown with blue stripes, see photo p. 20.

SEE ROCK CITY had its new borders!

I loved that there were two different border designs—yet another way to keep this re-imagined version from taking itself too seriously—and I thought of another passage from Dr. Berlo's book:

"Fallibility, irregularity, ambiguity, asymmetry. All fall short of 'perfection.' All exist in nature and art for a reason. They introduce something interesting, some conflict, something for the eye or mind to linger on."

The new plan was coming together and I could not stop smiling.

Sky fabric for Row One (January, February, and March)

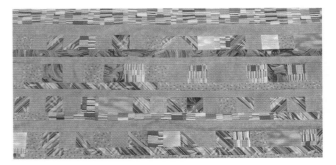

Sky fabric for Row Two (April, May, and June)

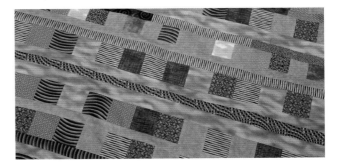

Sky fabric for Row Three (July, August, and September)

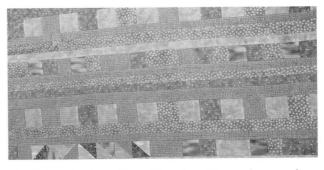

Sky fabric for Row Four (October, November, and December)

Considering leftover strips of four patches and pieces of strata

January block, version 3

January block, version 4

Once I finished removing the royal blue border strips, it was time to stop and assess:

❖ General plan for layout – check.

❖ Four yards of scrappy fabric for enlarging skies – check.

❖ Strips and scraps for enlarging, improving, and personalizing grounds – check.

❖ Inner and outer borders ready – check.

Armed with the necessary materials and excited to create a new and improved version of SEE ROCK CITY, I used the blocks in Row Four (October, November, and December) to determine the quilt top's targeted 80" width.

The never-quite-understood large half barn in January's block had to go, but I needed something tall in that spot to balance December's windmill. Brainstorming during a telephone conversation, Lynne and I were tossing out ideas—and there it was—a flagpole.

Using a fussy cut from a long-stashed fat quarter and a narrow strip of dark fabric, January's flagpole was quickly designed and installed. Version 4 was a keeper.

February's upgraded block looked even better with its enlarged scrappy sky and even scrappier ground.

March's block was upgraded with fussy cut chickens free pieced into a scrappy barnyard and a fussy cut rooster on a red plaid fence.

As one last nod to March's windy weather, a fussy cut kite was appliquéd onto the windy sky.

Using Row One's scrappy fabric sky panel, I cut and added strips to fill the areas above each barn's horizon line.

Using the scrappy ground fabrics, I pieced together strips and segments to fill in the areas below the blocks' existing grounds.

With great excitement, I lined up the horizons and pieced the first row together.

With minimal trimming, the row measured 19" tall x 80" wide.

I was thrilled to share this photo with my blog readers in early June.

Among the comments and e-mails, I found this one: *"I have to tell you that I am still seeing more of a structured/defined area around the barns than I would have thought you would do."*

I'm sure the writer wasn't the only one who wondered about the less-obvious but still clearly-defined block shapes within the new row.

February's block revised

March revisions

Row One reveal

Planning revisions for April

April revised

May revised

My response included this explanation:

"I did all of this because I wanted to get rid of that background fabric and the skinny dark blue border strips. I never actually said I was going to take each of the blocks completely apart – that just doesn't happen when they're free pieced. If using made-fabric had been my plan from the very beginning, you would have seen more of what you describe (less 'structured/defined area'). But since I had already free pieced the twelve individual blocks and THEN decided to use the made-fabric to enlarge and blend them together—yes, you are right—you can still see the outline of each block. I really wasn't trying to hide them.

Hopefully, things will make more sense once I get the other rows pieced and photographed so you can see more of what I already see in my head."

Moving on to Row Two, and sticking to my plan to "play more" and "work less," I fussy cut a flock of sheep for April's block.

The multiple scrappy free pieced fabrics made things SO much more interesting.

I enlarged the skies and barnyards for May. Allowing that one independent sheep to wander away from the flock made me smile.

(When I "smile" at something like this, it's because I can see the puzzle pieces coming together and feel things moving in the right direction.)

June's block was the easiest to upgrade needing only additional scrappy sky and ground.

With great joy, I shared this photo of Row Two on June 16. It measured 21" tall x 80" wide.

SO much better!

Quickly I pulled together the scrappy sky panel and ground fabrics for Row Three (July, August, and September). But after adding low stone walls and a fussy cut herd of dairy cattle, one of my design wall process photos brought things to a standstill.

New scrappy sky and ground for June block

Row Two revealed

The dark vertical strip in the transition between the July and August barnyards interrupted the horizontal visual flow. It had to go.

Patient unstitching allowed me to insert a more subtle and scrappier group of strips.

Detail photo of dark green strip

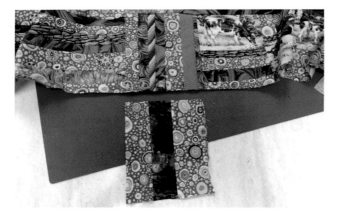

Out with the old and in with the new

High flying birthday balloons join party

Back on track, I added fussy cut bales of hay and more low stone walls to the September barnyard. I also appliquéd eight fussy cut hot air balloons before filling in the empty spaces above all three blocks' horizon lines with scrappy sky fabric.

Two short seams to attach the three blocks, a bit of squaring up, and Row Three, measuring 25" tall x 80" wide, was shared on the blog on June 20.

Fueled with enthusiasm, I moved on to Row Four (October, November, and December).

I did not have any Halloween novelty fabrics, so I asked Lynne to check her stash.

As luck would have it, Yvonne (who lives in Massachusetts) had sent Halloween scraps to Lynne for her FOUR SEASONS quilt. Lynne happily shared the remains of Yvonne's scraps allowing me to add a well-travelled trio of cheerful jack-o'-lanterns in front of October's barn.

The transition from October's deeply piled colorful leaves to December's dreariness definitely posed quite a challenge.

Row Three revealed

October's leaf-strewn barnyard with jack-o'-lanterns flanked by modern and vintage tractors

Ready to create November's ground fabric

Drab medium-brown strips became fading-autumn strata

After revising December's barnyard fabric choices, the fussy cut bright red bird perched on a stone wall was pieced in place in honor of my late mother's favorite bird and her too-close-to-Christmas birthday.

With much rejoicing, Row Four, measuring 27" tall x 80" wide, was shared on my blog on June 25.

Within days, the rows were sewn together and the 1¼" inner border and 5" outer borders were stitched in place.

And *then* I realized I was never going to be content with the sudden color change at the seam line between the November and December barnyards.

December revisions

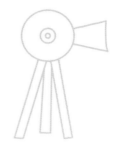

Row Four reveal

Planning a few subtle but necessary changes

Substitution work in progress

After playing around with leftover bits and pieces, I came up with a plan to substitute a softer blend of colors.

That plan meant carefully unstitching several seams INSIDE the finished quilt top in order to remove these four small pieces.

As I stitched the replacement strips in place, I kept hearing the voice of my grandmother, "If it's worth doing, it's worth doing well."

The seam softening alteration was definitely awkward, tricky, and time-consuming but, voice or no voice, it needed to be done.

Phase II came full circle on June 28 when the much-improved SEE ROCK CITY flimsy, measuring 81" x 100" was shared on my blog.

This time when I passed the top back to Chris, there were no doubts.

SEE ROCK CITY, 81" x 100", Designed and pieced by Julie Sefton.
Quilted by Chris Ballard, Oakland, Tennessee

Finishing
SEE ROCK CITY

Sneak peek of quilting in progress **PHOTO:** Chris Ballard

I n early 2013 Chris loaded SEE ROCK CITY onto Iris, her longarm machine.

From the very beginning of our working relationship Chris had cautioned me about potential pucker problems when using my beloved scrappy quilt backs. The topic of those conversations was no longer theoretical. It had become a real live crisis.

The "Godzilla Pleat" **PHOTO:** Chris Ballard

In hindsight, I should never have inserted those vertical and horizontal strips of multi-directional, heavily-seamed, scrappy-pieced strata into SEE ROCK CITY's back with such nonchalance. Due to the quilt's large size and the extensive, heavy custom, free motion quilting, a significant pucker (not so affectionately nicknamed "The Godzilla Pleat") had brought progress to a complete standstill.

The quilt was removed from the longarm machine and hours of intense telephone conversations left both of us badly shaken. Chris asked me to visit so she could show me the problem and discuss possible solutions. Ideas ranged from removing ALL of the quilting stitches so a replacement back could be substituted to the surgical removal of stitching in the affected areas in order to flatten the puckers and hand stitch them in place.

Spending those hours with Chris in her studio taught me more than all of our previous conversations added together. Understanding first-hand the nitty-gritty of her quilting process taught me in the most practical way possible why flat backs with straight edges are so important.

In the end, we agreed on a targeted approach. Chris spent hours removing thousands of quilting stitches in order to hand stitch the pucker's fullness into secure, flattened tucks. Finally, the quilt was loaded back onto her machine so quilting could resume.

SEE ROCK CITY triumphantly returned home on March 9, 2013. The quilt was "tamed" that same day. ("Taming" = trimming away the excess batting and backing in preparation for binding.) I had so much fun discovering the most delightful quilted details including a tail for the kite, bunting between the upper and lower stories of several barns, door frames and window panes, designs within the trees, board lines in the barns' siding, swirling gusts of wind, and ripples waving through the grasses.

I have included "before" and "after" photos for each of SEE ROCK CITY'S twelve barn blocks to illustrate the almost magical transformation that can take place when a free pieced top is quilted, pp. 30–33. My hope is that these side by side comparisons will encourage bolder fabric choices and creative design decisions while reducing scrap-anxiety and overall stress levels. Take time to study how the quilting stitches soften those previously obvious seam lines. Consider how the quilted textures add continuity, movement, and dimension. Notice how the quilted details add visual interest and personality, inviting a closer look.

Encouraged by the many positive responses to the newly-completed quilt, I submitted an entry for AQS Grand Rapids 2013 and I was thrilled when SEE ROCK CITY was juried into the show.

The quilt was also entered, juried into, and displayed during 2014 AQS Quiltweek® Phoenix, Lancaster, Paducah, Charlotte, Chattanooga, and Des Moines; as well as Albuquerque and Syracuse 2015. And ALL of this was possible because the free piecing process allowed me to translate my love of barns into a very special quilt.

Author with SEE ROCK CITY, AQS Quiltweek® Grand Rapids 2013 PHOTO: Larry Sefton

> Many people have asked me: "So how long did it take you to make that quilt?"
>
> My answer? "A lifetime."
>
> "Why? What do you mean?"
>
> "Everything I have ever seen or done has made me who I am now – and who I am now impacts the quilts I make."

January block (before)

January block (after quilting)

February block (before)

February block (after quilting)

March block (before)

March block (after quilting)

April block (before)

April block (after quilting)

May block (before)

May block (after quilting)

June block (before)

June block (after quilting)

July block (before)

July block (after quilting)

August block (before)

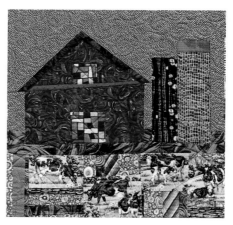

August block (after quilting)

September block (before)

September block (after quilting)

October block (before)

October block (after quilting)

November block (before)

November block (after quilting)

December block (before)

December block (after quilting)

One of my favorite photos of the quilt. PHOTO: Julie Sefton

Introduction to the Seasonal Sampler Project

Weathered and overgrown West Tennessee barn
PHOTO: Sammie Ballard

Now it is YOUR turn!

The process notes that follow show how to build four different styles of barns, one for each of the four seasons. By setting all four blocks together, you will create a one-of-a-kind SEASONAL SAMPLER.

These techniques will then allow you to create many other types of free pieced buildings including aging or deserted industrial buildings, general stores, fishing villages, one room school houses, country churches, grand houses, humble bungalows, seaside cottages, or any other design style you choose.

Whether representational or purely from your imagination, the construction choices are YOURS!

Materials

The tools and supplies I keep close at hand include the following:

- ❖ My camera (process photos allow you to record a variety of layout ideas to compare your options)
- ❖ New rotary cutter blades
- ❖ Sharp straight pins
- ❖ Extra sewing machine needles
- ❖ Several pre-wound bobbins of thread (I typically use a medium gray 50-wt.)
- ❖ 6" x 12" and 6" x 24" quilting rulers
- ❖ Blank and lined paper, colorful pens and highlighters, mechanical pencils, and a good eraser.
- ❖ Small bins or boxes for saving/sorting usable scraps/trimmings
- ❖ A lint roller
- ❖ A trash can in each work area to make clean up easier

General Notes

Free piecing is not a quick and easy project—it is a relational process, not a prescribed method.

Making an extended series of design decisions takes time and energy. So does finding your own rhythm.

Be prepared to change your mind – more than once.

Free piecing does not always progress in a tidy linear manner. Think of it in terms of building a jigsaw puzzle. Try a piece here, try another piece there, and keep fitting pieces together until the finished block (usually larger than you anticipated) eventually reveals itself.

Concrete silo not far from my house, circa 1920

If things are not working, get up and walk away, especially if you are frustrated or angry. Taking a break can be exactly what you need in order to move forward. Creativity needs room to breathe, so know when to get out of the way.

To help assess the relative sizes of the various pieces and parts of your work, try using painter's tape on your design wall or floor to outline the general size of the block you want to create. Being able to glance up and see your desired space can be helpful.

Use your camera to capture details and color combinations that catch your eye. I keep images like these in digital "gestation files."

If you have not read Austin Kleon's books *Steal Like an Artist* and *Show Your Work*, I highly recommend them. Keeping your eyes and mind open to the millions of ideas you encounter every day can add so much to your own creative efforts.

Try very hard not to compare your "beginning" to the "middle" and "advanced" of others, particularly when you are online or at quilt shows. Absorb those gathered observations but also give yourself time to find YOUR own style.

Preparation
One

"Listen to your broccoli and your broccoli will tell you how to eat it" is a nonsensical phrase from a Mel Brooks movie. In our case, it should read: "Listen to your quilt and your quilt will tell you how it wants to be made." Listen to your own creative voice, NOT the voice of your inner critic. Do you like what you're making? If so, keep going. If not, stop and identify what it is that you don't like.

Ask yourself what it is that makes you uncomfortable. Be specific and make sure you are able to clearly describe your discomfort using words. This process allows you to clarify the issue so you can take steps to resolve the problem.

Two

Working from a scrappy perspective seriously reduces the stress that comes from the inevitable question, "Do I have enough of that fabric?" I am sure I am not the only one who has over-purchased or underestimated how much fabric is needed for a special project. I much prefer to use a mix of fabrics from my own stash to generate scrappy sewn-together or made-fabric.

If your yardage is in doubt, choose at least three different fabrics that play well together and consider using them as one. If you are unsure about this approach, look back at the scrappy skies in SEE ROCK CITY. Single fabric skies are perfectly okay, but scrappy skies almost always invite a closer look.

A caution about directional fabrics. They can be very effective, but be sure each piece is correctly oriented before you stitch it in place. (Remember that "correctly oriented" can be whatever you choose it to be, not necessarily so that things match or line up.)

Three

Press well after every seam. No excuses. I press using steam, but the choice is yours.

Keep the back of your work neat. Trim your threads and use your ruler/rotary cutter to remove excess fabric after sections are seamed together. I have worked "messy" and I have worked "neatly" and the results speak for themselves. Consistent attention to these

Fabrics from my stash for consideration

More fabrics pulled from stash for SEE ROCK CITY's second layout

West Tennessee barn, notice the contrasting sunny and shady areas in the grassy field, the sky's wispy clouds and contrails, the barn's gambrel roof line and prominent hay hood, the left annex's fence, and the barn quilt above the large center door.
PHOTO: Chris Ballard

Aging 1940s barn on working farm near Memphis, Tennessee

housekeeping details will be greatly appreciated by your quilter. In fact, some quilters actually refuse to accept "messy," thread-covered work.

SQUARE VS. TRIM? In this book, SQUARE means to straighten uneven edges and TRIM means to reduce the size of your fabric's dimensions. Example: SQUARE to keep your working edges straight and even but TRIM only when it is time to reduce the overall size of your block or remove excess fabric after joining two larger sections together.

DO NOT TRIM too soon. I cannot over-emphasize this. Keeping that excess fabric in place will dramatically increase your future design options. Trimming at the last possible moment also protects the edges of your fabric from fraying and distortion caused during repeated handling.

DO NOT SKIMP when cutting fabrics. Oversize pieces ensure you will have enough fabric for necessary seam allowances. The excess can always be trimmed away later, but there is nothing more frustrating than coming up short.

When you do need to trim away excess fabric, be careful to position your ruler over your stitched block. If your rotary cutter happens to slip, it will most likely veer away from the ruler into the excess fabric and not into your newly-pieced work.

IF you cut or trim something too small, do not automatically toss it aside. In some cases, you can resolve the problem by adding more fabric. The extra seam lines, and even a different but related fabric, add texture and interest.

Four

Most of all, I want you to use, I mean *really use*, your book.

Take it to an office supply store or copy shop, ask them to slice away the spine, and have them replace it with a coiled binding (typically black, but sometimes there are color options). Why? The inexpensive coiled binding allows your book to lay flat and stay open.

Dedicate this book to yourself. Using colorful markers, write your name boldly on the inside cover along with the date and where you are from. Maybe include a favorite quotation (or two). Embellish your dedication by adding colorful doodles or quilting motifs to personalize the blank spaces. Physically and mentally claiming this book as your own removes an invisible but powerful barrier and gives you the freedom to actually use all of this information.

Design Inspiration

As you consider barns to take inspiration from, notice the details and think about the fabrics in your stash. Think about color but also think about the texture, shading, value, and patterns of your fabrics. What do each of the seasons look and feel like where you live? How could you isolate elements or combine multiple fabrics to convey a particular idea?

Skies do not always have to be blue—they can feature multiple shades of purples, violets, golds, oranges, and grays. Night skies are another possibility. Grounds can, of course, be manicured golf course green. They can also be covered with colorful wildflowers or patches of unkempt weeds.

Think carefully about what surrounds the barn. Is there a large tree with a tire swing? What about mountains in the distance or even a fishing pond? Are there tiny details you'd like to include? Don't forget to use the capabilities of your sewing machine.

How to cope with all these details and ideas? Keep a note pad and pencil in your car and in your purse/travel bag. Take your camera when you go out to run errands or simply use your phone's camera. Send yourself a text or email or leave yourself a voice mail. Use the GPS in your car or phone to capture a "you are here" location for reference. Create a labeled "ideas" box for your studio and an "ideas" folder on your computer. Use one or all of these to capture those moments of inspiration.

Rear wall of multi-level barn in Henniker, New Hampshire, notice multiple color variations on rear wall, ground mixture of rock, stone, grass, and gravel with changes in elevation, dense trees, and contrasting window frames   PHOTO: Julie Sefton

SEASONAL SAMPLER Notes

Like SEE ROCK CITY, the SEASONAL SAMPLER blocks feature the colors and shapes of western Tennessee.

Here, the ground closest to the barn tends to be more landscaped so I typically use a single fabric close to my buildings. My barnyards and fields are then filled with seasonally-appropriate scrappy colors. Whether you prefer scrappy fabric close to your building or a single fabric for your ground area—the choice is yours.

Prior to creating the barns in SEE ROCK CITY, the free pieced buildings I had seen were designed with the roof fabric stitched directly to the sky fabric. However, since many barns have interesting, dimensional roof lines and multiple materials like corrugated metal, weathered wood, and asphalt shingles, I started inserting strips of contrasting fabric between roof and sky to suggest that mix of shadows and textures.

I have included some of the work-in-process measurements for the SEASONAL SAMPLER barns, but these bracketed side notes are for reference only. Your barns can be any size you choose.

Remember, you can also mix your techniques to create the effect you want. Quilters have been combining techniques to achieve their creative visions for years. I no longer do much handwork thanks to my arthritic thumb joints, but my limitation should not stop you from using your full range of skills.

Most of all, have fun personalizing your barns.

Barns and silos near Walpole, New Hampshire, notice classic red with white trim color scheme, textures of double silos, clouds layered across the sky, and rutted gravel road **PHOTO:** Lynne Tyler

This 1940s wisteria-covered brick silo stands on a 20-acre tract, surrounded by upscale housing and medical offices, just a few blocks from Interstate 240 in Memphis, Tennessee. **PHOTO:** Julie Sefton

Details on barn near Jackson, Tennessee, notice hooded double haymow openings, use of vertical and horizontal siding boards, and shapes created by white trim boards.
PHOTO: Julie Sefton

Storage building near Brasstown, North Carolina, notice color of the roof, texture of the open-slatted horizontal siding, open windows, and weathered gray vertical door boards
PHOTO: Julie Sefton

Grain silos near Covington, Tennessee **PHOTO:** Larry Sefton

SEASONAL SAMPLER, *68" x 55"*
Designed and pieced by Julie Sefton.
Quilted by Chris Ballard, Oakland, Tennessee

SPRING

**Block size:
22" x 26"**

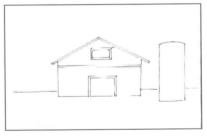

S pring's block includes a fairly symmetrical, windowless two-story barn with simple roof lines, a haymow sign, silo, and scrappy barnyard.

Make a quick sketch to help clarify your ideas. You do not need to create a detailed architectural plan, pattern, or template. Your drawing is for general reference only and chances are your barn will evolve far beyond whatever you sketch (fig. 1).

Fig. 1. Working sketch for spring barn

Gather a wide variety of fabrics for your barn, sky, and ground. You will not use all of them, but working from a larger group makes the selection process easier and a lot more fun (figs. 2a and 2b). Play around with possible fabric combinations until you chance upon one that makes you smile—that's when you know it is time to begin (fig. 3, p. 46).

Important Note: When considering a single fabric for the sky, I select pieces that are a full yard or more.

Fig. 2a

RIGHT: Figs. 2a and 2b. Fabrics were pulled from stash for consideration, most measure less than a yard and several are small scraps (perfect for windows, doors, accents)

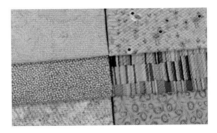

Fig. 2b

Fig. 3. Testing edited fabrics together

Fig. 4. Partially framed sign

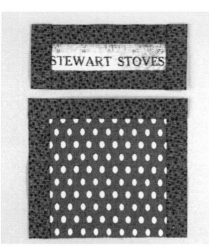

Fig. 5. Framed barn door and sign

Details

I like to start with one of the detail elements. Sometimes that element is the doorway. Other times I use windows or signs. Since each aspect of the barn needs to be relative in terms of proportion and scale, I start small and build from there.

1. Frame your sign using narrow strips of a contrasting fabric (fig. 4). I cut wider strips, knowing it is easier to trim them down later. From a "finished" standpoint, I prefer thinner framing over wide framing, but feel free to experiment to see which style you prefer.

2. Finalize your choice of doorway fabric and cut to size, making sure to add seam allowances. *(In this case, I started with a 5" square.)*

3. Frame the doorway by cutting and stitching strips of contrasting fabric to the right and left sides of the door followed by a full-width strip across the top (fig. 5).

Using a single fabric to frame the door(s), window(s) and/or sign(s) adds an element of consistency, but only if you feel so inclined.

Building the Lower Story

1. Using your framed doorway as reference, stitch sections of fabric to the right and left sides of the door. Use pieces that are almost twice as wide as you think you'll need – you can always trim them down later.

2. Measure the width of your door with side pieces attached. Cut a full width strip of barn fabric and stitch it across the top, again making sure the strip is tall enough to allow for trimming later. (fig. 6). *(My framed door measured 5 ½" tall, so I added two 6" x 8" side pieces and a 5" full width strip across the top.)*

3. Cut two long strips of your roof line fabric now so they are ready to use as you experiment with design options.

Creating the Upper Story

1. Cut upper story fabric for the right and left sides of your framed sign, making sure the finished width is at least equal to the width of your lower story. Stitch in place. *(I added two pieces each 2 ½" tall x 8" wide.)*

2. Cut two full width strips of fabric to fill the areas immediately above and below the sign, making sure the finished width is at least equal to the width of your lower story. Stitch both of these pieces in place. *(My strips were 2 ½" tall x nearly 20" wide.)*

3. If you want to include a strip of contrasting color between the upper and lower stories of your barn, cut a narrow strip, making sure the finished width is at least equal to the width of your lower story. Stitch the strip to the lower edge of your newly-assembled upper story (fig. 7).

4. Using your lower story to gauge the relative height and width needed for your upper story, cut and stitch another full-width strip to the upper edge. If you don't have enough to cut a single large piece, you can use several narrower strips, either full width or in staggered lengths.

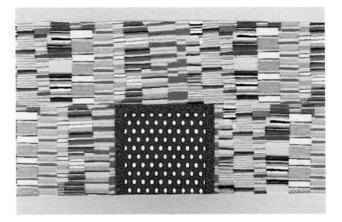

Fig. 6. Assembled lower story

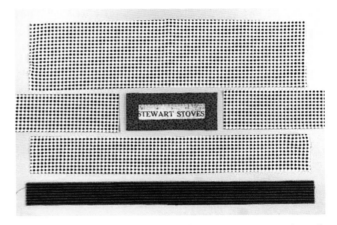

Fig. 7. Shown are fabrics cut for steps 1, 2, and 3 of Creating the Upper Story.

Trim excess threads to keep back of your work neat

Fig. 8. Experimenting with angles using roof line fabric strips

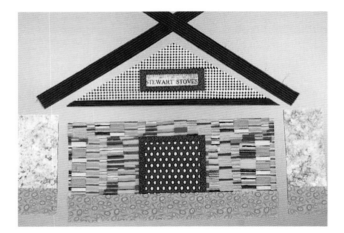

Fig. 9. Two sky/ground strips prepared for lower story

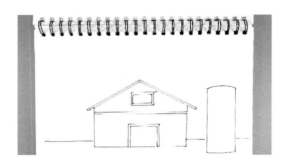

Test possible layout options using your upper and lower stories and roofline strips (fig. 8). Small adjustments can make a big difference! Once you are happy with your layout, trim the upper edge of the lower story as needed, making sure to include seam allowances. If you cut off too much, do not despair—cut another strip, stitch it in place, and move on. DO NOT stitch the stories together yet.

Adding Sky/Ground Strips to Lower Story

Important Note: This step is critical if you want your roof to overhang your building.

1. Finalize your choices for sky and ground fabrics.

2. Cut a strip of ground fabric measuring at least 2½" x 6"–8" wider than your lower story.

3. Cut two pieces of sky fabric each 3"–4" wide and equal to the height of your barn's lower story.

4. Cut two (2) segments from your ground fabric strip, stitching one (1) segment to each piece of sky fabric (fig. 9). Test potential shapes/ dimensions using the upper/lower stories, roofline strips, and sky/ground fabrics. Use process photos to record your layout ideas. Take your time and experiment until you are happy.

5. Trim the roof line edges of the upper story, making sure to include seam allowances.

6. Sew roof line strips in place.

Before stitching the sky/ground combination, use your sky fabric yardage and spend a few minutes experimenting with design options. Consider variations in the thickness of the rooflines, the amount of upper story overhang, and how each decision will influence the final width of the lower story and the overall look of the barn.

Figure out whether you want your barn to sit on top of the ground (meaning you would line up the ground seams) or nestle down into it by raising the side strips (fig. 10). By shifting the horizon line of the sky/ground strips, your barn can sit level, lean at a deliberate angle, or appear to be built on a hill.

7. Trim the sides of your lower story, making sure to include seam allowances.

8. Cut and stitch a 2½" strip of ground fabric along lower edge of barn's lower story. Trim ends as needed to line up with the barn's sides.

9. Stitch the two sky/ground strips from step 4 to the right and left sides of the lower story, positioning as desired.

10. Stitch the upper and lower stories together but DO NOT TRIM SIDES. The sides need to extend far enough to be stitched into the extended roof line/sky fabric seams in the next section (fig. 11).

Adding Upper Sky Sections

1. Cut an oversize triangle from sky fabric for the right side of your block. DO NOT SKIMP. Stitch in place, making sure the lower end of seam extends across sky fabric at right side of lower story AND beyond the roof's peak. Press, but DO NOT TRIM (fig. 12).

2. Cut another oversize triangle from sky

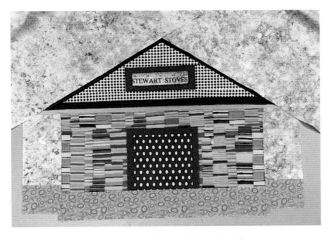

Fig. 10. Large sections of sky fabric laid atop upper story to gauge scale, lower story shown with barn set below horizon line (steps 7–9)

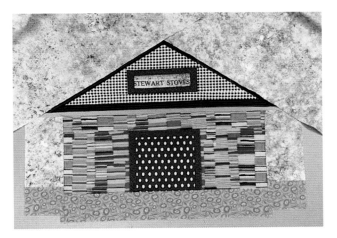

Fig. 11. Upper and lower stories stitched together

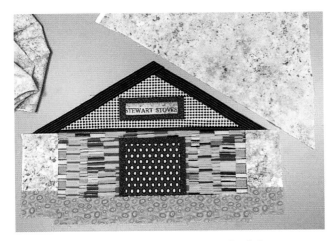

Fig. 12. Testing right side's oversize sky fabric triangle

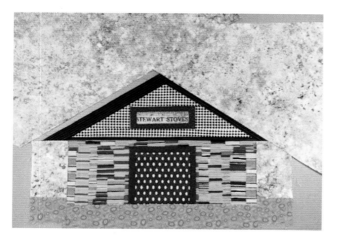

Fig. 13. Testing left side's oversize sky fabric triangle

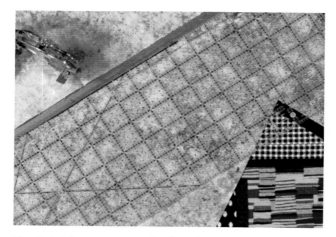

Fig. 14. Note position of ruler, if rotary cutter slips, it will be more likely to veer into excess fabric and away from block

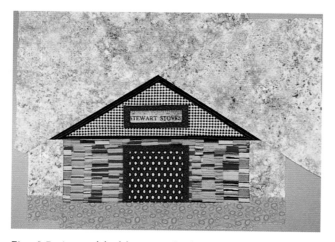

Fig. 15. Assembled barn with sky attached

fabric for the left side of the roof. Again, DO NOT SKIMP. Stitch in place, making sure the lower end of the seam extends across the sky fabric on the lower story's left side AND across the sky fabric above the roof's peak. DO NOT TRIM (fig. 13).

3. Press, then flip the left side triangle back over the barn. Carefully trim excess flap of fabric from the right side's triangle. See figure 14 for suggested ruler position.

Adding a Silo

1. Cut a rectangle in proportion to your barn. (*Mine measured 3½" x 8½".*)

2. Cut and stitch a piece of ground fabric to the lower edge of your silo rectangle. If your ground fabric is directional, double check the orientation before stitching.

3. Cut and stitch a strip of sky fabric to the upper edge of the silo rectangle, making sure the sky extends all the way to the top of your existing barn block.

4. Cut and stitch together a strip of sky fabric and segment of ground fabric, as shown on the far right in the photo above, making sure the sky fabric extends all the way to the top of the block (fig. 16).

Experiment with horizontal and vertical positioning of the silo next to the barn. Do you want your silo level with the lower edge of the barn's lower story OR do you want your silo to appear closer (as shown figure 17 with the ground line lower) or farther away, in which case the ground line would need to be higher?

5. Trim right edge of the barn block, making sure to retain the seam allowance. Stitch silo strip in place, adjusting position of lower edge as desired

6. Stitch the additional strip of sky/ground fabric from step 4 to the right side of the silo, adjusting the horizon line as needed.

Adding More Ground

1. Trim and square the block's upper edge.

2. Measure the distance between the roof's peak and the upper edge of the block. This will help you determine how much ground you want to add to balance the block's overall dimensions. (*My block has 5" of sky showing above the roof's peak.*)

3. Square the lower edge of your block and determine how much ground you want to add. (*I chose to add approximately 4½" of ground.*)

4. **Option A:** Cut additional ground fabric as desired. Stitch to lower edge of block.

5. **Option B:** To create a scrappy barnyard as shown here, gather an assortment of companionable ground fabrics. Stitch two small pieces together. Press and square.

Stitch two more pairs together. Press and square.

Repeat, adding additional pieces as needed, to achieve desired size (fig. 18).

Stitch completed scrappy ground panel to lower edge of block.

6. Square edges of the finished block, but DO NOT TRIM away any excess fabric.

7. Carefully stay stitch the perimeter of your block to help prevent bias edges from stretching and seams from coming apart.

Fig. 16. Adding a silo

Fig. 17. Experimenting with silo assembly positioning (shown with pieces laid in place prior to seams being stitched)

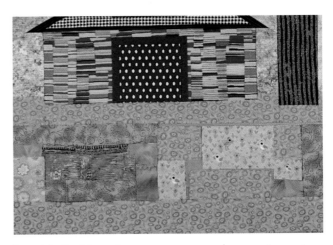

Fig. 18. Building the scrappy ground, one piece at a time

SUMMER

Block size:
33" x 24"

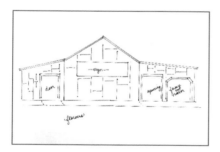

Fig. 1. Working sketch for summer barn

Fig. 2. Fabrics under consideration

S ummer's barn features two side annexes or bays, an arched open doorway to showcase a fussy cut tractor, two additional door openings, a sign, angled roof lines, scrappy sky fabric, and scrappy strata ground.

The building's shape was inspired by the aging barn shown on page 40. Another of that farm's buildings (shown on page 12) was recently torn down, encouraging me to honor this unsung reminder of the area's heritage. The flower strewn barnyard was inspired by another nearby farm that supplied area florists for many, many years before being sold to a commercial developer.

Selecting Fabrics

These colors from my stash reflect the intensity of our area's summertime with deeper blues, darker greens, and vivid reds. Explore your stash to see which fabrics speak summertime to you, trying not to impose too many intellectual restrictions (fig. 2).

Another way to consider the fabrics from your stash is to fold them and lay them out in the approximate positions they would occupy in the block. Using this approach, you can experiment to your heart's content—arranging and rearranging before cutting into your fabric (fig. 3).

Scrappy Strata for the Flower Fields

1. Cut a number of equal width strips from your green fabrics. *(Mine were cut at 2")*

2. Stitch these green strips together end to end to form a single long strip.

3. Trim the long strip into any length greater than the anticipated width of your block. *(Mine were cut at 40")*

4. Cut a variety of small pieces from floral fabrics into slightly narrower but equal width strips. *(Mine were cut at 1½")*

5. Stitch these floral strips together end to end to form a single long strip.

6. Trim the long floral strip into whatever width you chose in step 3.

7. Pair and stitch together a green strip with a floral strip.

8. Continue stitching pairs together until you have created a single large piece of scrappy green-floral strata (fig. 4).

Fig. 3. My "fold-and-lay-into-position" technique

Fig. 4. Assembled ground strata

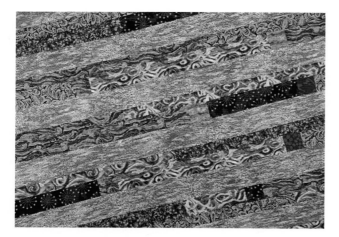

Fig. 5. Summer sky strata

Fig. 6. Farm implement yardage

Fig. 7. Fussy cut tractor stitched between door frame strips

Scrappy Strata for the Skies

For the scrappy skies, I used a variety of blue strips cut in 3 different widths. (*I cut mine at 1½", 2", and 2½".*)

1. Stitch each group of equal width strips together end-to-end to create a single long strip.

2. Cut each long strip into lengths longer than the anticipated width of your block. (*I cut mine at 40".*)

3. Pair and stitch these strips together again and again until you have a single large piece of scrappy sky strata (fig. 5). (*I first paired a 1½" strip with a 2" strip, before pairing the combined strip set with a 2½" strip.*)

Set the sky and ground fabric aside for now.

Arched Open Doorway for Right Bay

1. Fussy cut a farm implement of your choice to be pieced inside the barn's right bay doorway, making sure to include additional fabric on all sides (fig. 6).

2. Stitch narrow strips of framing fabric to the right and left sides of the fussy cut tractor (fig. 7). (Stitching your framing strips close to the fussy cut tractor suggests the tractor is further inside the barn.) DO NOT TRIM.

3. Square the upper edge, making sure to leave enough for a seam allowance.

4. Cut two shorter pieces of framing fabric, making sure the pieces are wide enough to extend beyond the outside edges of the doorframe after they are flipped and pressed. Stitch these pieces on an angle across the upper inside corners (fig. 8).

5. Square the upper corners. Experiment with spacing options, then cut and stitch another strip of framing fabric across the full width of the doorframe's upper edge.

6. Trim the visible width of your framing strips as desired. *(I trim to a generous ½" which yields a ¼" frame when the element is pieced into the barn wall.)*

7. To complete the look of the open arched doorway's frame, cut two rectangular pieces of barn fabric. Each piece should be wide enough to extend beyond the outside edges of the doorframe after they are flipped and pressed. Stitch these pieces on an angle across the upper OUTSIDE corners of the doorway's framing (fig. 9).

8. Square the top and sides only of the completed doorframe. Trim framing strips to your desired width, making sure to include seam allowances.

DO NOT TRIM the bottom edge – you will need the excess later.

Sign and Two More Doors

1. If desired, select a fussy cut element to represent a sign for the barn's center section.

2. Frame your sign element (sides first, then top and bottom). Trim the sign's framing to your desired width, making sure to leave enough for seam allowances (fig. 10). Set the framed sign aside.

Fig. 8. Arched doorway framing strips before trimming to final size

Fig. 9. Trimmed arched door opening after addition of barn fabric at upper corners

Fig. 10. Completed sign and door elements

Fig. 11. Right bay assembled but not trimmed

IF YOU CHANGE YOUR MIND

In a move that is so typical of the free pieced process, I changed my mind when it came time to install the previously-made red door into the barn's left bay. The red door's print blended too far into the barn's red plaid, so to create the higher contrast look and feel of rusty corrugated metal, I chose a warm golden-brown tonal fabric with uneven rows of horizontal dots.

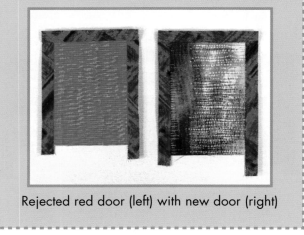

Rejected red door (left) with new door (right)

3. Finalize your choice of fabrics for the open doorway in the barn's right bay and the large door in the barn's left bay. Frame each of these doors.

4. Trim the framing strips around both doors as desired, making sure to leave enough for seam allowances.

Assembling the Right Bay

1. If you want the upper edges of your two doorframes at different heights, cut and stitch a slightly wider strip of barn fabric to the top of whichever doorframe you want to appear shorter. (*I added this wider strip above the arched doorframe on the right, making sure the plaids did NOT match.*)

2. Cut a strip of barn fabric to fill the space between the two doors. Stitch this narrow strip of barn fabric to the right side of the open doorframe. Square the upper edge to match the upper edge of the open doorframe.

3. Cut and stitch a strip of barn fabric above the open doorframe and narrow connecting strip. Square and trim the right and left sides as needed

4. Align the doorframes as desired, then stitch the right side of that narrow connecting barn fabric strip to the left side of the arched door opening.

5. Cut and stitch a strip of barn fabric to the right side of the arched doorframe.

6. Cut and stitch a strip of barn fabric to the left side of the assembled doorway unit. Square the upper edge of this assembled doorway unit.

7. Stitch a wide band of barn fabric across the full width of the assembled doorway unit. DO NOT TRIM the sides (fig. 11).

Press unit well but DO NOT TRIM the lower edges of the right bay.

Set the right bay aside for the time being while you assemble the left bay.

Assembling the Left Bay

1. Cut and stitch a narrow strip of barn fabric to the right side of the doorframe.

2. Cut and stitch a large chunk of barn fabric on the left side of the doorframe.

3. Cut and stitch a wide ("tall") strip of barn fabric across the upper edge of the door unit.

4. Square the top and sides, but DO NOT TRIM the lower edges (fig. 12).

Set the left bay aside.

Center Section, Lower Story

1. Cut and stitch strips of barn fabric to the right and left ends of your framed sign. Consider changing the orientation of the barn fabric to add visual interest.

2. Square upper and lower edges.

3. Cut and stitch a large, full width segment of barn fabric to the lower edge of the sign strip.

4. Cut and stitch a large, full-width segment of barn fabric to the upper edge of the sign strip (fig. 13).

Fig. 12. Assembled but untrimmed left bay with door

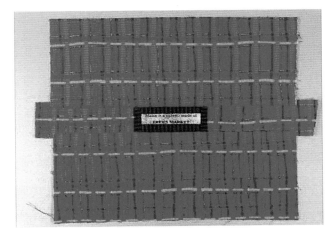

Fig. 13. Oversized center section of lower story

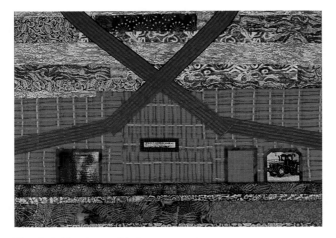

Fig. 14. Playing with layout options

Fig. 15. November's quilted barn from SEE ROCK CITY, full quilt on p. 29

Fig. 16. Left and right bays with "gravel" ground strips in place

DO NOT TRIM or square this unit yet. Allow it to remain oversize.

This excess fabric will give you "wiggle room" as you make additional design choices and finalize the layout of your barn.

Considering Design Options

1. On a large flat surface, arrange your sky and ground fabrics, both side bay units, and the center section of the lower story.

2. Decide on the fabric for your roof lines and cut several 1½" strips. Use these roof line strips to experiment with different roof line angles, remembering that you will add additional barn fabric for the upper story later (fig. 14).

3. If you find the colors and textures too distracting to visualize your roof lines, use sheets of paper or large pieces of neutral fabric to temporarily cover or crop away the surrounding sky and/or barn fabrics. The goal is to be able to clearly see your desired shapes.

4. Consider potential locations for the seams that will join the side bays to the barn's center section. Do you want one bay to be wider than the other or do you want them to be symmetrical? Do you want the side bay roof line angles to match or do you want them to be different? Take some time to play with layout possibilities.

Make notes about your desired measurements and/or take process photos for reference. You'll have additional opportunities to revisit these choices.

Refining the Three Lower Story Sections

Before working with your barn's lower story units, notice the narrow strips in a contrasting green on the right and left sides of the center section in See Rock City's November barn (fig. 15). These strips were added to help define the vertical edges between the barn's three sections. Later, different quilting stitch designs further emphasized this distinction.

Also notice the slight shift in the alignment of the center section's lower edge. Nesting the center section deeper into the ground fabric was done to suggest that the barn's center extends forward into the barnyard, ahead of the side bays.

In case you want to incorporate these subtle techniques, I've included notes for them below.

1. Square the lower edges of both side bays

2. Stitch narrow strips of ground fabric to lower edges. DO NOT TRIM the lower edge. (*I chose to insert a narrow layer of gravel between the barn and the ground fabric, figure 16.*)

3. Square the inside edges only of both bays, leaving enough for seam allowances.

4. Using the side bays and your notes, determine the desired width for your barn's center section. Trim right and left sides of center section as needed, making sure to include seam allowances.

5. If desired, cut and stitch narrow contrasting strips to right and left sides of the center section. Trim strips as desired.

6. Cut and stitch a narrow strip of ground fabric to the lower edge of the barn's center section, squaring ends only as needed. (*Again, I chose to insert a layer of gravel here.*)

7. Trim the lower edges of ground fabric strips on all three sections of your barn to an equal width. (*My strips were trimmed to ½" so that ¼" would be visible after the final seams were stitched. I sometimes refer to this resulting look as "visible width.*")

8. Stitch a wider strip of ground fabric to the lower edge of each bay and the barn's center section (fig. 17). (*I cut these strips in the 3" range.*)

More Decisions

1. Using the various barn components, determine how much of the barn's fabric you want visible above the sign in the center lower story. Trim the upper edge of the center lower story as needed.

2. Using the two side bay units and your roof line strips, determine your angles. Pin roof line strips in place, but DO NOT stitch yet.

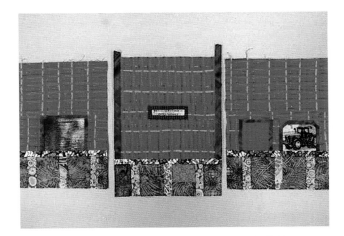

Fig. 17. Strata stitched to lower edges of all three lower story sections

Fig. 18. Roof lines and supporting sky/ground fabrics stitched in place on side bays

Fig. 19. Completed left side bay unit

Fig. 20. Completed right side bay unit

Finalizing the Side Bay Units

1. In order to create air space for the roof's overhang, cut two strips of sky fabric, making sure each is slightly taller than the height of the side bay.

2. Cut and stitch an equal-width piece of ground fabric to one end of each sky fabric strip.

3. Position these combination strips along the exterior/outside edge of each side bay.

4. Stitch sky/ground pieces in place, adjusting horizon line as desired.

5. Stitch roof line fabric strips in place, continuing seam across the upper edge of sky/ground fabric strip (fig. 18).

6. Carefully trim upper edges to remove excess sky fabric.

7. Square outer edges, making sure to include seam allowances and roof line overhang. Trim only if desired.

8. Cut and stitch together two wider sky/ground strip combinations, making sure each one is tall enough to reach slightly above the top edge of the roof AND wide enough to be included in the seam line that will attach the sky fabric above the roof line to the lower story as shown (fig. 19). Stitch one combination strip to the outer edge of each side bay as shown (*I cut my strips 3"*).

9. Cut wide strips of sky fabric/strata to upper edge of each side bay's roof line. DO NOT SKIMP.

Make sure the upper strip is wide enough so it can be trimmed square with the interior (upper) corner of each side bay (figs.19 and 20).

10. Stitch sky strips in place. Press seams well and square upper edges.

Before moving on, take a few minutes to lay out all three sections of your barn's lower story. Square and trim the interior vertical edges as needed (fig. 21).

Center Section, Upper Story

1. Cut an oversize segment of barn fabric to use for the center barn's upper story, making sure it is large enough for potential roof line angles.

2. Using pieces of your sky and roof line fabric as a guideline, finalize the shape of upper story. Consider changing the orientation of your upper story fabric to add visual interest (fig. 22).

3. Trim roof line angles as desired. If you are uncertain, use a chalk pencil to mark the inner edge of the roof line strips onto the upper story fabric. You can then use the chalk lines when trimming the upper story angles, making sure to add seam allowances.

4. Cut and stitch roof line fabric strips in place (fig. 23).

While making yet another visual check, I decided to add a narrow strip of framing fabric across the upper edge of the center lower story. (As you will see in later photos, this last-minute addition ended up being trimmed away.)

Adding the Sky

1. Cut an oversize triangle of sky fabric for the right side of the block, making sure the triangle extends from the side of the outside

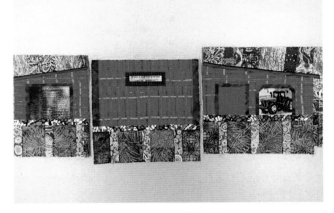

Fig. 21. Considering final width adjustments

Fig. 22. Considering upper story roof line options using fold-and-lay-in-place technique

Fig. 23. Completed upper story and lower story sections

Fig. 24. Overlapping right and left sky triangles laid in place before stitching

Fig. 25. Left side sky triangle laid in place to test positioning after attaching right side sky triangle

Fig. 26. Right and left side sky fabric stitched in place

edge of the right bay to well above the peak of the upper story's roof. DO NOT SKIMP.

2. Cut an oversize triangle of sky fabric for the left side of the block, making sure it is large enough to extend from the far left side of the left bay to the upper edge of the right side sky (fig. 24). DO NOT SKIMP.

3. Stitch the upper story and the right side sky triangle together (fig. 25). DO NOT TRIM.

4. Stitch the left sky triangle to the upper story (fig. 26).

5. Flip left side triangle back to reveal the excess fabric from the right side's triangle. Trim as needed using the seam allowance as your guide (fig. 27).

6. Press sky seams flat.

Assembling the Upper and Lower Stories

Experiment with alignment options for the completed upper and lower stories, then stitch the full width horizontal seam (fig. 28).

Fig.27. From reverse side trim away excess fabric

Adding Additional Ground Fabric

1. Square upper edge of sky fabric, but DO NOT TRIM excessively.

2. Square lower edge of ground fabric. Determine how much additional ground fabric needs to be added to balance the sky.

3. Cut additional ground fabric as needed and stitch to lower edge.

4. Press well and square all edges, but DO NOT TRIM excessively (fig. 29).

Fig. 28. Completed upper and lower story units ready to be stitched together

One Last Change of Heart

After the block was completely finished, I decided to remove the dark horizontal strip between the upper and lower stories of the barn's center section.

Here are the steps I took to make that happen.

1. I unstitched the long horizontal seam between the upper and lower stories.

2. I trimmed ¾" from the lower story's upper edge, thus removing the framing fabric strip.

3. The upper and lower sections were then seamed back together (fig. 30). See finished block page 48.

Remember—be sure to stay stitch the edges of your completed block to protect seams from coming apart or bias edges from being stretched during handling.

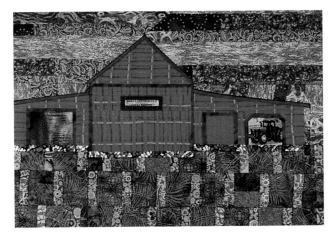

Fig. 29. Completed block before final adjustment

Fig. 30. Detail of revised horizontal seam

AUTUMN

Block size: 28" x 27"

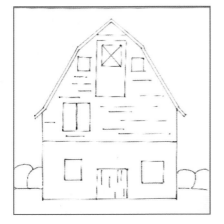

Fig. 1. Working sketch for autumn barn

The third barn for the SEASONAL SAMPLER features windows (framed and unframed), an elongated haymow opening (a mow—which rhymes with "cow"—is the loft where piles of hay are stored), and a gambrel roof (a ridged roof, each side of which has two slopes). In addition to your fabrics for the barn, you will need at least a yard of one fabric for the sky and an assortment of autumn-colored fabrics for the scrappy leaf-strewn ground. Check your stash for the colors of autumn where you live. Keep playing with possible combinations until you discover the group that makes you shout "YES!"

Making Scrappy Ground Strata

The following steps share yet another variation on how to make scrappy strata.

1. Cut narrow equal width strips from several autumn-themed fabrics (fig. 3). (*I cut mine in random lengths but all 1¼" wide.*)

LEFT: Fig. 2. Edited group of fabrics arranged in approximate positions

2. Trim strips to equal lengths, saving the odd-sized trimmings from the strip ends. (*I cut mine 12" long.*)

3. Sort these lengths into contrasting pairs, then stitch each pair together end to end.

4. Stitch a contrasting odd-size trimming to one end of each pair.

5. Stitch all joined strips together end to end, creating one very long strip.

6. Trim the long single strip any length that exceeds the anticipated width of your block. (*I trimmed mine to 36".*)

7. Sort and stitch lengths into scrappy pairs, stitching side to side this time (fig. 4).

8. Repeat pairing and stitching process, pressing after each seam, until you have assembled one large piece of scrappy strata. Set this aside for later.

Creating the Lower Story

1. Choose a fabric for the barn door. Cut an oversize square. (*Mine was cut in the 4½" range.*)

2. Frame the sides and top of the door using narrow strips of contrasting fabric. (*Mine were cut at 1" and were not trimmed down.*)

3. As you choose fabric for the barn's small windows (two on the lower level and two near the haymow opening), consider whether you want the windows to suggest interior light radiating outward, dark dull surfaces, or the illusion of texture. Cut four smallish squares. (*Mine were cut at 2½" and trimmed down later.*)

Fig. 3. Strips cut for scrappy ground

Fig. 4. Scrappy ground strata

Fig. 5. Fabric segments cut for lower story

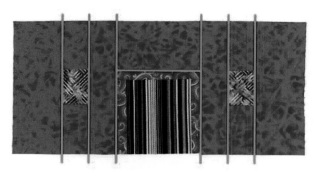

Fig. 6. Fully assembled lower story

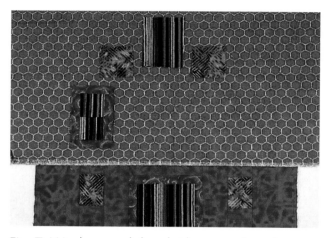

Fig. 7. Windows and door laid on top of yardage

Fig. 8. Sub-units for upper story

4. Cut several strips of barn fabric and subcut into segments as illustrated in figure 5, p. 63. *(Mine were cut at 2½" with a 3" strip for the outside edges and the space above the barn's door.)*

5. Stitch barn fabric to upper and lower edges of unframed window squares.

6. Stitch segment of barn fabric to upper edge of framed door unit.

7. Adjusting width as desired, stitch strips of barn fabric to the right and left sides of the barn door unit.

8. Adjusting width as desired, stitch window strips to right and left side of barn door unit.

9. Stitch remaining barn fabric strips to right and left sides of door/window unit (fig. 6).

10. Square, but DO NOT TRIM, upper and lower edges.

The Upper Story Begins

The tall upper story will be constructed in layers. The framed windows, access door, and elongated haymow door/opening will be created first. These elements will then be pieced into a series of horizontal strip units. The strip units will then be seamed together to create the oversize upper story. As you work, use the lower story unit to check and adjust spatial relationships to YOUR liking (fig. 7).

1. Cut a rectangle (or two smaller pieces seamed together) for the upper story's access door. Frame this rectangle using narrow strips of contrasting fabric, adjusting width and height as desired.

(My finished door was originally cut at 2½" x 4" and later trimmed to 1½" x 3". The framing strips were cut at 1¼" and later trimmed to a visible ½" width.)

2. Frame the second set of window squares using narrow strips of contrasting fabric, adjusting width as desired. *(Mine were cut 2" x 2½" and trimmed to 1½" wide x 2¼" high before framing.)*

3. Cut rectangle of fabric for haymow door. Cut an equal width strip of upper story fabric and seam to door's lower edge. Note the subtle difference in texture by changing the fabric's orientation.

4. Trim this seamed unit to desired size, making sure to include seam allowances. *(Mine was cut at 3" x 9" and trimmed to approximately 2½" x 7¼" before framing.)*

5. Frame the sides of this trimmed unit using narrow strips of contrasting fabric.

6. Adjust height as needed, then frame upper and lower edges.

7. Lay your framed window and door units on top of the barn's uncut upper story fabric. Consider alignment and layout options, making sure to include the lower story as you experiment (fig. 8).

8. Measure the width of your barn's lower story. In the following sequence of steps, you will be using this measurement plus 2" (referred to as a "full-width strip") to cut several horizontal strips from the barn's upper story fabric. *(My barn measured 16" so I cut my full-width strips at 18".)*

9. Cut a full-width strip to form the upper story's lower edge. *(I cut mine 2½" wide.)*

10. Cut a full-width strip equal in height to your framed access door unit. Subdivide this strip in order to insert the door unit. *(My strips were cut at 4½" and trimmed to size once the door unit was inserted.)*

11. Cut a narrow full-width strip as a spacer between the upper edge of framed access door and the lower edge of the framed haymow door/opening (fig. 9). *(I cut my strip 1½" wide.)*

12. Assemble pieces from steps 9-11, trimming horizontal edges as needed. DO NOT TRIM sides (fig. 10).

Fig. 9. Strips from steps 9–11 for upper story

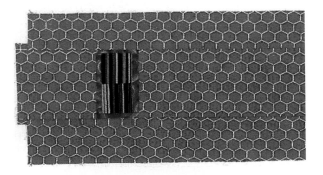

Fig. 10. Sewn strips after completing step 12

Fig.11. Segments described in steps 13 and 14

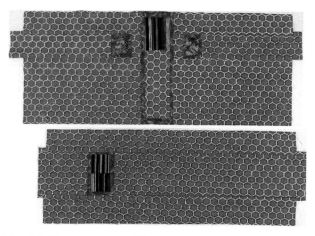

Fig. 12. Two sections of barn's upper story

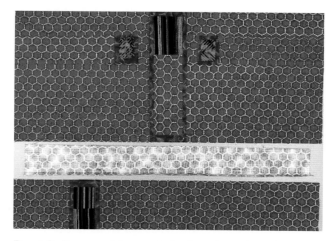

Fig. 13. Spacer strip unstitched and ready to be removed

13. Cut a full-width strip equal in height to your framed windows. Subdivide as shown in figure 11. *(My strips were cut at 3" to allow for trimming after all seams were stitched.)*

14. Cut a wider full-width strip to fill the space between the lower edge of the framed windows and the lower edge of the framed haymow door/opening unit. Subdivide as shown in figure 12. *(Mine were cut at 7".)*

15. Cut an additional narrow full-width strip. Fold in half crosswise and cut along fold (fig. 13).

16. Stitch seams for right and left window strips, trimming horizontal edges as needed.

17. Stitch lower edge of left window strip to one half of wide strip.

18. Stitch upper edge of left window unit to one section of narrow strip.

19. Stitch lower edge of right window strip to remaining half of wide strip.

20. Stitch upper edge of right window unit to remaining section of narrow strip.

21. Stitch left side unit to left side of framed haymow door/opening unit, adjusting alignment as desired.

22. Stitch right side unit to right side of framed haymow door/opening unit, adjusting alignment as needed to coordinate with the left side window's placement.

23. Position the two assembled sections of your barn's upper story on a flat surface. Experiment to see how you want to join the units including horizontal and vertical alignment relationships, making sure to also consider the barn's lower story.

24. Trim horizontal edges as needed. (At this point, I realized my barn did not need the additional spacer strip between the upper edge of the access door's framing strip and the lower edge of the haymow door/opening segment, so it was removed, fig. 13.)

25. Seam together the two upper story sections.

26. Cut a wide strip of fabric for the upper story peak area. I chose to introduce a different fabric for this strip (fig. 14).

27. Stitch wide peak area strip to upper edge of upper story. DO NOT TRIM THE SIDES.

28. Experiment with different roof line fabrics. Once you make a decision, cut at least 2 long strips (fig. 15).

29. Using a large flat surface, layer your sky fabric, ground strata, lower story, and upper story. Use the roof line strips to experiment with spacing and angles. If you cannot clearly visualize your spacing and angles, use a large piece of neutral fabric or sheets of paper to reduce the visual distraction of surrounding sky and barn fabrics. Once you are happy with the arrangement and general shape, make some notes regarding dimensions and take a couple of photos for easy reference.

Enlarging the Lower Story

1. Determine the desired width and height for your lower story. Trim sides as needed (fig. 16).

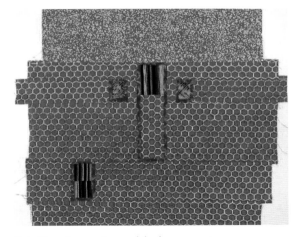

Fig. 14. Caption – Assembled upper story

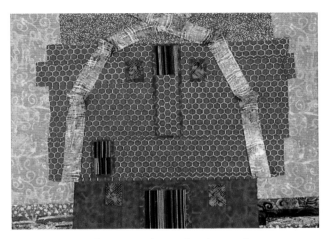

Fig. 15. Considering a shape for the roof

Fig. 16. Sky and ground pieces for the lower story

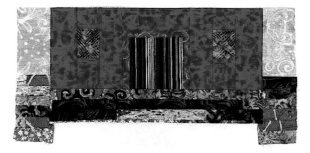

Fig. 17. Updated lower story

Fig. 18. Considering modifications

Fig. 19. Making necessary adjustments

2. Cut two pieces of sky fabric at least 2½" wide x the height of the lower story.

3. Cut two pieces of ground strata at least 2½" wide as shown above. Stitch one piece of ground strata to each of the two strips of sky fabric.

4. Cut a 2½" strip of ground strata and seam this to the lower edge of the barn's lower story.

5. Position and stitch sky/ground strips to right and left sides of the barn's lower story (fig. 17).

Use the newly updated lower story to re-evaluate your barn's overall layout. Experiment with spacing options below the lower edge of the access door, various roof line angles, and potential roof overhang spacing. Be sure the look of the barn makes you happy.

Lower Story Revisions

Looking back at the working sketch (fig. 1, p. 62), two major issues were clear. The access door in my barn was too close to the left roof line, and the roof lines were supposed to stop near the top of the access door instead of extending all the way to the lower edge of the upper story's fabric.

Additional sky yardage was folded around the updated roof shape to help visualize the barn's eventual shape (fig. 18). I also cut two additional strips of sky fabric and positioned them on either side of the barn to hide the too-long roof lines.

1. Unstitch the horizontal seam between the access door strip and the haymow door/opening strip IF you want to retain the lower edge of the haymow opening's frame. Otherwise, simply slice the sections apart (fig. 19).

2. Trim the access door strip to match the lower story's width adding ½" for seam allowances (fig. 20).

3. Stitch strips of sky fabric to right and left sides of the access door strip.

4. Determine desired distance between the lower edge of the access door and the upper edges of the lower story's window and door frames. Trim as needed.

5. Using the roof section, do a quick double check for alignment and relational spacing.

6. Stitch the lower story and access door strip together (fig. 21).

7. Set the newly revised lower story aside for now.

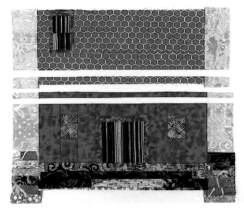

Fig. 20. Trimming to size

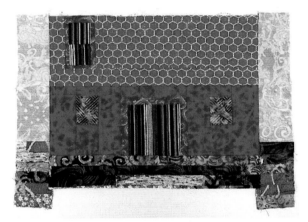

Fig. 21. Lower story revised

Upper Story Roof Lines

The gambrel roof design features two angles on each side of the building. I refer to these as the "peak angle" and the "lower angle."

1. Using the roof line fabric strips, finalize your choice of roof line angles. Pin the strips in place, using the inner edge to indicate future seam lines. Make sure you allow enough width across the lower edge for the roof's overhang (fig. 22).

(Because I wanted to maintain the symmetry of this barn's roof, I used a chalk pencil to lightly mark the seam lines. For a liberated barn, I would proceed without marking the seam lines.)

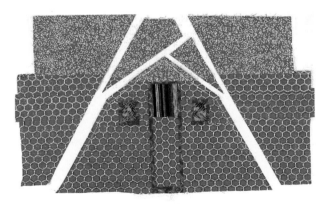

Fig. 22. Upper story shape emerges

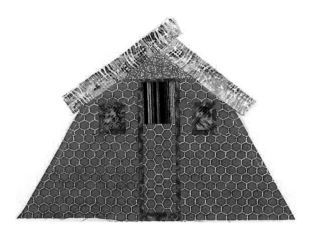

Fig. 23. Right and left peak angle roof line strips sewn in place

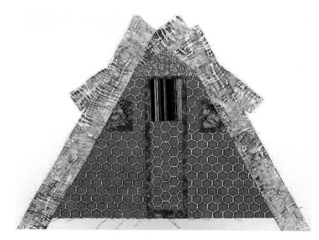

Fig. 24. Lower angle roof line strips sewn in place

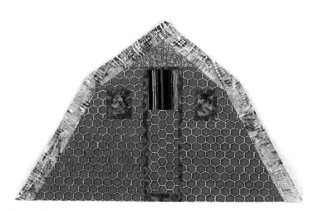

Fig. 25. Roof section trimmed

2. Carefully trim away excess roof fabric, making sure to keep your seam allowances. Handle this now-bias-edged piece with care.

3. Stitch the right side peak area's roof line strip in place and flip/press.

4. Stitch the left side peak area's roof line strip in place, making sure it is long enough to extend across the right side's strip. Flip and press (fig. 23).

5. Stitch the right side's lower roof line strip in place, making sure it extends across the right peak angle strip's width.

6. Stitch the left side's lower roof line strip in place, making sure it extends across the left peak angle strip's width (fig. 24).

7. Flip both roof line strips and press carefully, making sure not to stretch or distort the fabrics.

8. Square roof line strips, taking care to remove the overlaps beneath the top layer, but DO NOT TRIM just yet (fig. 25).

Adding the Sky

The four pieces of sky fabric will be added in this order:

One – Peak angle, left side ("sky section one")

Two – Lower angle, left side ("sky section two")

Three - Peak angle, right side ("sky section three")

Four – Lower angle, right side ("sky section four")

1. Cut an oversize rectangle for the upper left peak area. DO NOT SKIMP (fig. 26).

(Consider where the extended seam lines for the subsequent sections of sky fabric will be. If necessary, cut a larger rectangle for this upper left-hand area.)

2. Stitch sky fabric rectangle to upper left peak angle roof line (fig. 27).

3. Flip and press, but DO NOT TRIM.

4. Cut a large oversize rectangle for the left lower angle (sky section two). Before stitching, double check that the full length of the seam line will extend beyond the upper edge of sky section one AND ALSO extends below the lower edge of the barn section.

5. Cut a larger rectangle if needed, then stitch sky section two in place (fig. 28). Flip and press.

6. Working from the back with your ruler positioned over the upper story, trim away excess fabric from sky section one (fig. 29).

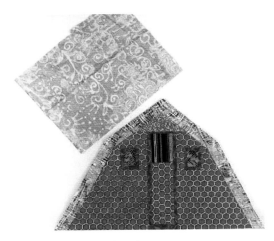

Fig. 26. Rectangle for sky section one

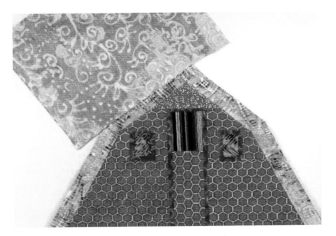

Fig. 27. Sky section one stitched in place

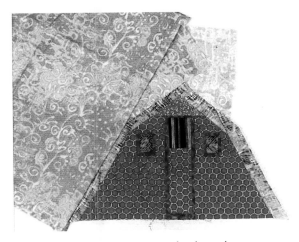

Fig. 28. Sky section two stitched in place

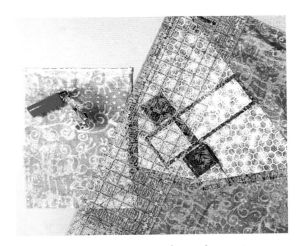

Fig. 29. Preparing to trim excess from sky section one

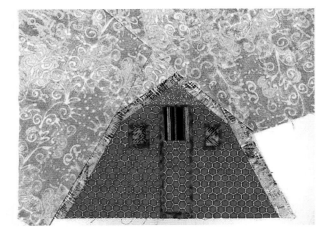

Fig. 30. Sky section three stitched in place

Fig. 31. Sky sections one, two, three, and four stitched in place

7. Do a quick double check before proceeding.

8. Cut and test fit an oversize rectangle for the right peak angle area (sky section three). Double check that the full length of the seam line will extend across and beyond the seam line and upper edge of sky sections one and two. If necessary, cut a larger rectangle.

9. Stitch sky section three in place (fig. 30). Flip and press.

10. Again, working from the back with your ruler positioned over the upper story, trim away excess fabric from sky sections one and two.

11. Using the same approach, cut and test fit an oversize rectangle for the right lower angle area (sky section four) – double checking that the full length of the seam line will extend across and beyond the upper edge of sky section three. If necessary, cut a larger rectangle.

12. Stitch sky section four in place (fig. 31).

13. Working from the back with your ruler positioned over the upper story, trim away excess fabric from sky section three.

14. Turn the upper story with its newly attached sky fabric right side up.

15. Square the edges but DO NOT TRIM.

16. Do another visual check using your upper and lower story sections but do not stitch them together.

If you want to include trees in your block, visit http://thefreepiecedbarnproject.blogspot.com and look for the Tutorial tab.

Editing Your Work

Arrange your lower story, upper story, and ground strata on a large flat surface. If you are planning to make the four block Seasonal Sampler, include your spring and summer barns in the visual conversation to see how the three blocks work/play together. If you love what you've created, congratulations. However, when I studied my autumn block alone and in context with the others, three significant issues demanded action.

Issue One? The tree was simply too small and too dark.

Solution? Make a different tree or remove the tree from the block (fig. 32).

Issue Two? The leafy ground was much too dull and dreary.

Solution? Replace the browns with shades of orange.

Issue Three? The barn was several inches too tall in context with the spring and summer blocks.

Solution? Find a way to shorten the barn without sacrificing its essential character.

1. I first folded a tuck into the upper story so the roof line overhang lined up with the upper edge of the access door (fig. 33).

2. Next, I added a second folded tuck to raise the upper edge of the lower story, thereby eliminating the entire spacer strip stitched below the access door (fig. 34).

Fig. 32. Considering potential barn elements on design wall

Fig. 33. Upper story folded under for minimal roof line overhang

Fig. 34. Lower story folded to reduce area below access door

Fig. 35. Access door strip unstitched from lower story

Fig. 36. Shortened upper story with lower story after access door strip removed

Fig. 37. New ground strips sewn in place

I liked this version of the barn itself, but within the sampler-related layout, the composition was still not working well. Later, after my head cleared, the solutions were obvious. I needed to completely remove the tree, shorten the lower portion of the upper story, and completely remove the access door and its strip. With those three goals in mind, it was time to renovate.

Let the Renovations Begin

1. Unstitch or slice away the horizontal seam joining the lower story to the access door strip (fig. 35).

2. Double check the new relationship between the lower story and the upper story (fig. 36).

3. Remove the sky/ground strips from the sides of the lower story.

4. Remove the full-width ground strip from the lower edge of the lower story.

5. Prepare new sky/ground strips for the sides of the lower story. Refer back to Enlarging the Lower Story (pp. 67–68) if you need additional guidance. *(I cut my strips 4"–5" wide.)*

6. Prepare and stitch a new full-width ground strip across the lower story's lower edge (fig. 37). *(I cut this strip 3" wide.)*

7. Stitch new sky/ground strips to the right and left sides of lower story. (The upper story was still too tall, so I trimmed another inch off the lower edge.)

8. Stitch upper story and lower story together, centering the haymow door above the barn's lower story door and adjusting alignment so roof lines overhang the side walls of the lower story (fig. 38).

9. Square right and left sides from upper edge to lower edge.

10. Keeping the sampler layout in mind, compare the autumn block's width with the width of the spring block. If the autumn block is considerably narrower, cut and stitch in place additional sky/ground strips as needed. *(In my case, the autumn barn was wider so no extra strips were needed.)*

11. Determine how much additional ground fabric is needed.

12. Prepare or cut additional ground fabric as needed. Stitch additional ground fabric in place along lower edge of block. Square edges but DO NOT TRIM excessively (fig. 39). *(I chose to fill the revised barnyard with scrappy made-fabric.)*

Fig. 38. Renovated barn

Fig. 39. Nearly completed autumn block

Hay Bales (optional)

Inspired by a farm an hour south of where we live, I decided to include a fence row of circular hay bales. If you would like to include hay bales, check your stash for hay-color fabric, remembering that the rolling spiral design of the bales can be added or emphasized during the quilting process (fig. 40).

Fig. 40. Yardage for fussy cutting

Fig. 41. Fussy cut pieces before final trimming

Fig. 42. Choosing thread color for appliqué

1. Using scissors, cut out two likely groups of hay bales (fig. 41).

2. Select a thread color that blends into the hay bales (fig. 42).

3. Adjust alignment as desired, then appliqué hay bales in place using your preferred technique. *(I chose to set my hay bales below the horizon line and used a narrow zig-zag stitch to machine appliqué.)*

4. Stay stitch the outer edges of your block to protect your bias edges and prevent your seams from coming apart (fig. 43).

Congratulations! In addition to completing the third of your four SEASONAL SAMPLER blocks, you have also learned several ways to consider and make work-in-progress edits to your free pieced design (fig. 44).

Fig. 43. Outer edges of hay bale stay-stitched

Fig. 44. Autumn block with hay bale fence rows

WINTER

Block size: 31" x 25"

Fig. 1. Working sketch for winter barn

Fig. 2. Digging a little deeper into the stash

Where I live, December and January are filled with dormant, khaki-colored grasses, and skies that alternate between shades of gray and pale, washed-out blues. Whether you live where the winter months are warm and green or cold and snowy, select fabrics with a range of colors and textures to illustrate what you see outside your windows.

This block's weathered barn features a gambrel roof with double roof lines, a seasonal wreath above the cross-timbered double doors, a split rail fence, a trio of sturdy silos, and scrappy yet neutral ground cover.

At first, I thought about building my weathered winter barn with a hand dye stripe and setting it on a stone foundation. I also thought about a pale blue batik sky and two silos, one in paisley and the other in chevrons, but that overall look felt flat and dull. I went back to the stash and added a few more options. This time, the mix of textures and colors spoke more clearly to my vision (fig. 2)—which meant it was time to begin.

Fig. 3. Initial strip inserted into double doors

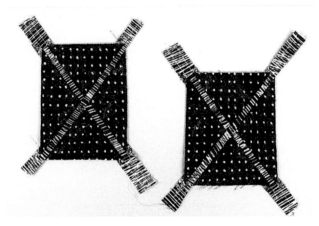

Fig. 4. Completed inserts for cross-timbered double doors

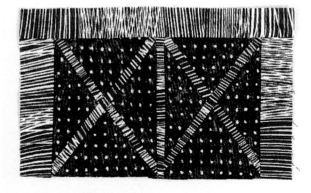

Fig. 5. Framed double door unit

Cross-Timbered Double Doors

1. Cut two oversize rectangles for the barn's double doors. (*I cut mine in the 4" x 6" range.*)

2. Cut four strips of your chosen framing fabric. (*I cut mine 1¼" wide, then trimmed them to ½" visible width after steps 4 and 6.*)

3. Slice both rectangles diagonally from upper left corner to lower right corner.

4. Stitch framing strip to one edge of the left triangular section of each door's rectangle. Flip and press, trimming inserted strip to desired width. DO NOT TRIM the ends of the inserted strip (fig. 3).

5. Stitch the upper triangular section of each door's rectangle to the second side of the inserted framing strip, being careful to align the pieces so they create a rectangular shape when flipped and pressed.

6. Repeat Steps 3, 4, and 5 slicing both door rectangles from lower left corner to upper right corner, across the previously inserted strip (fig. 4).

7. Stitch a narrow framing strip to the right hand side of the left door. Trim strip to desired width, but do not trim the ends.

8. Stitch the left edge of the right door to the vertical framing strip, forming a single double door unit.

9. Square double door unit, removing ends of inserted strips. Trim double door unit to desired size, making sure to add seam allowances.

10. Stitch narrow framing strips to right and left sides of double door unit (fig. 5).

11. Stitch narrow framing strip across the upper edge of double door unit. Square, but DO NOT TRIM.

Framed Haymow and Optional Seasonal Wreath

1. If desired, prepare fussy cut seasonal wreath by stitching pieces of the barn's fabric in place as needed.

2. Cut a square piece of fabric for the haymow's opening. *(I cut mine 3½" square.)*

3. Stitch narrow strips of framing fabric to the right and left sides of the haymow square.

4. Stitch narrow strips of framing fabric to the upper and lower edges of the haymow square.

5. Square edges, then trim framing fabric to desired width, making sure to include seam allowances (fig. 6). *(I trimmed these to ¾" visible width, cut at ¾" so ½" showed after the seams were stitched, just slightly wider than the ½" visible width framing strips for the double doors, cut at ½" so ¼" showed after the seams were stitched.)*

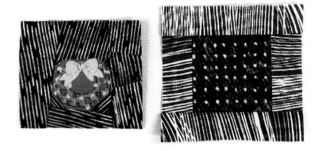

Fig. 6. Fussy cut wreath framed with barn fabric (left) and framed haymow opening (right)

Scrappy Strata for the Ground

1. Finalize your choice(s) for ground fabric(s).

2. If desired, cut strips to desired width and piece scrappy strata, using your preferred method (fig. 7).

Suggestion: Small pieces of stone print fabric suggest the presence of rocky outcroppings in your barnyard or fields.

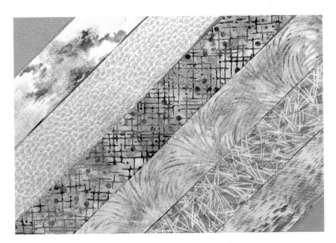

Fig. 7. 2½" strips cut to make ground strata

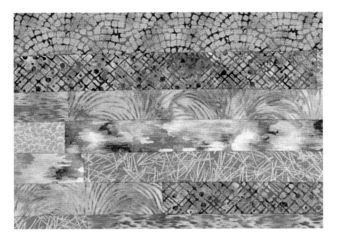

Fig. 8. Strata ready for use

Fig. 9. Possible fabrics for double roof line strips and silos

For the winter sampler block, my strips were sewn together end to end. The resulting single strip was then cut to equal size lengths. Those lengths were randomly stitched into pairs. The pairs were then randomly paired together as needed to create a single large piece of neutral scrappy ground (fig. 8).

Items to Consider Before Proceeding

1. Narrow your choices for the roof line fabrics.

2. Narrow your fabric choices for the silos. My initial plan was to include two banded silos as shown figure 9. Do you want to add the contrasting strip to one or both of your silos? (*I added a third silo to the group later in the process, adding the contrasting band only to the tallest of the three.*)

3. Consider whether you want to use a single fabric or scrappy strata along the horizon line and the lower edge of your barn. Do you want a combination of the two or do you want to introduce a third layer of stone or gravel?

4. Finalize your choice of fabric(s) for the sky.

Split Rail Fence

1. Cut a number of narrow strips from your desired fencing fabric. Plan to make your fence row longer than you are likely to need as you'll want it to extend beyond the left edge of your block. (*Mine were cut 1" wide and I used the framing fabric for visual consistency.*)

2. Cut several wider strips of sky fabric to fill in the areas above, below, and between the fence rails (fig. 10).

3. Create two horizontal strip sets, each with a fence rail strip stitched above a sky fabric strip. *(To reduce bulk, I pressed these lengthwise seams open.)*

4. Trim upper edge of lower strip set's fence rail to desired width, making sure to include seam allowance.

5. Trim lower edge of upper strip set's sky fabric, making sure to include seam allowance.

6. Stitch two horizontal strip sets together lengthwise.

7. Subcut prepared horizontal strip set into sections as shown figure 11, choosing width to suit the scale of your block.

8. Stitch one upright fence rail to the right side of each sub-cut section.

9. Trim upper edge of upper horizontal fence rail to desired width, making sure to include seam allowances.

10. Stitch a wider strip of sky fabric across the upper edge of the upper horizontal fence rail (fig. 12).

Suggestion: Cut this sky fabric strip wide enough so it is taller than the anticipated height of your barn's lower story. Otherwise, you will need to add another horizontal strip later in the process.

11. Trim lower edge of fence unit as desired, using the barn's double doors to verify that the size of your fence suits the scale of your block.

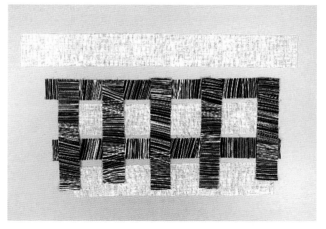

Fig. 10. Strips cut for split rail fence construction (shown here laid in place on top of sky fabric strips)

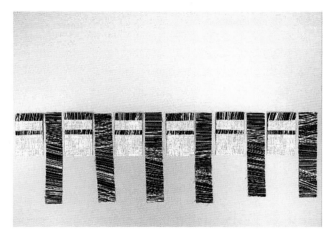

Fig. 11. Paired horizontal strip set sub cut for insertion of uprights

Fig. 12. Completed fence unit ready to be stitched to horizon line strip

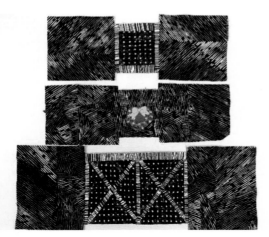

Fig. 13. Lower, middle, and upper units prepared for barn's three layers

Fig. 14. Four layers laid out prior to stitching

12. Attach a wide strip of your desired ground fabric along the lower edge of your completed fence unit.

Constructing the Upper and Lower Barn Units

The fabric used for the winter barn's weathered walls was pieced together using scraps of leftover batik.

1. Using the barn's double door unit as a guide, cut two oversize pieces of fabric for the barn's lower level. Stitch one oversize piece to each side of the double door unit. DO NOT TRIM.

2. Using the optional seasonal wreath element as a guide, cut two oversize pieces of fabric for the barn's second level. Stitch one oversize piece to each side of the prepared wreath unit (fig. 13). (If you elected not to include the wreath element, cut a single wide strip of fabric for this level.) DO NOT TRIM.

3. Using the framed haymow unit as a guide, cut two oversize pieces of fabric for the barn's peak area. Stitch one oversized piece to each side of the haymow unit. DO NOT TRIM.

4. Cut an additional oversize piece of fabric for the peak area above the haymow opening.

5. Square upper and lower edges on each of the barn's four horizontal layers (fig. 14).

6. Stitch two lower levels together, trimming upper and lower edges as desired before stitching. DO NOT TRIM the sides.

7. Stitch two upper levels together, trimming upper and lower edges as desired before stitching. DO NOT TRIM the sides.

8. Before joining the upper and lower story units, take a few minutes to experiment with the shape for your gambrel roof lines. Also consider your preferences for the visible width of each layer (fig. 15).

9. After using the upper and lower stories and your chosen roof line fabric strips for guidance, trim lower edge of upper story as desired.

Set the upper story unit aside while you complete the block's lower level.

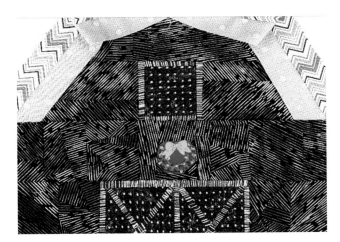

Fig. 15. Considering roof line angles

Assembling Block's Lower Unit

1. Trim upper and lower edges of barn's lower level as desired, making sure to include seam allowances.

2. Stitch a wide strip of ground fabric to the lower edge, trimming ends as needed.

3. **Left side** – double check desired position for the fence row unit, trimming only the right end as desired. Add additional sky and ground fabric to upper and lower edges as needed, making sure the fence unit is slightly taller than the barn's lower story and ground strip.

4. **Right side** – prepare a vertical combination strip of sky and ground fabric, adjusting the horizon line as desired. Double check to be sure this combination strip is slightly taller than the barn's lower story and ground strip. This combination strip is necessary if you want your roof to overhang the lower story on the right side (fig.16).

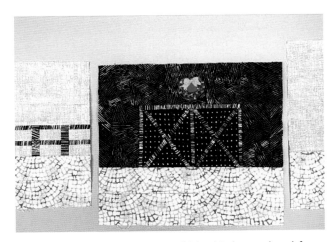

Fig. 16. Preparing sections of block's lower level for assembly

Fig. 17. Using inner layer of roof line strips to determine roof angles

Fig. 18. Adding the outer layer of roof line strips

Fig. 19. Sky fabric sections stitched in place

5. Stitch prepared fence row unit to left side of barn's lower story, positioning horizon line as desired.

6. Stitch the prepared sky/ground combination strip to the right side of the barn's lower story, positioning horizon line as desired.

7. Square the upper edge of the assembled lower story.

DO NOT TRIM right or left outer edges.

Upper Story Roof Angles and Roof Line Strips

For more detailed process notes on gambrel roof lines, please refer to the Upper Story Roof Lines (pp. 71–72) directions of the Autumn block.

1. Finalize desired roof angles using roof line strips as guides (fig. 17). Trim upper level as needed.

2. Stitch inner roof line strips in place, using the process described in steps 3–6 of the Autumn barn block (p. 72).

3. Trim visible width of inner layer strips as desired.

4. Attach outer layer of roof line strips (fig. 18), again referring to steps 3-6 of the Autumn barn block (p.72) .

5. Trim visible width of outer roof line strips as desired, making sure to include seam allowances.

6. Square lower edge of assembled upper story (fig. 19).

Adding Sky Fabric

For detailed process notes, please refer to the Autumn barn block (pp. 72–74).

1. Cut and stitch in place each of the four sky fabric sections.

2. Trim away excess fabric as needed.

3. Square the lower edge. DO NOT TRIM sides or upper edge just yet.

4. Verify how much additional sky fabric needs to be added to make the upper story's left side sky area as wide as the assembled lower story's left side.

5. Cut and stitch this additional sky fabric in place, trimming away any excess from the back side (fig. 20).

6. Square lower edge of upper story unit.

DO NOT fill in the right side of the sky – it will be filled in after the silos have been added.

7. Stitch upper and lower story units together (fig. 21). Square only the right side for now.

Adding the Silos

1. Cut an oversize rectangle of contrast fabric for each silo.

2. If desired, cut an oversize rectangle of fabric to band the upper edge of your silo(s) (fig. 22).

Fig. 20. Completed left sky area

Fig. 21. Assembled left (fence) and center (barn) sections

Fig. 22. Considering silo options using the fold-and-lay-into-position technique (explained in the summer barn introduction, p. 53)

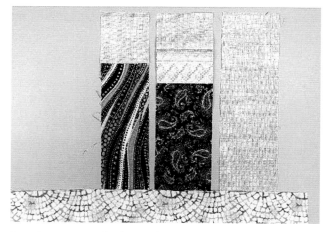

Fig. 23. Trimmed silos with ground strip laid over lower edges

Fig. 24. Silos stitched together. Note that I changed out the contrasting fabric on the taller silo in order to increase the level of contrast

Fig. 25. Instead of using the combination strip prepared in step 7, elected to add a third silo to the group

3. Trim each silo to desired width, making sure to include the seam allowances (fig. 23).

4. Add sky fabric to the upper edge of each silo.

5. Add ground fabric to the lower edge of each silo. (*I chose to align the lower edges of both silos. They can also be offset or staggered.*)

6. Prepare a wide strip of sky and ground fabric to fill the area on the right side of the right hand silo.

7. Depending on the size and arrangement of your barn block, prepare another narrower strip of sky/ground fabric to fill the area between the barn and the silos.

8. Stitch the silos together, adjusting lower edges as desired (fig.24). DO NOT TRIM upper or lower edges of the combined unit.

9. If desired, prepare another silo, following the procedure described above (fig. 25).

10. Stitch third silo or the combination strip from step 7 to the left side of the prepared pair of silos.

11. Square upper edge of combined silo unit.

12. Using the barn block and the silo unit for reference, prepare additional sky fabric to fill the area above the silos. Square left side and lower edge.

13. Stitch prepared sky to upper edge of silo unit. Square left edge.

14. Aligning the horizon line, stitch prepared silo/sky unit to the barn block (fig. 26).

Adding Scrappy Ground Strata

1. Trim and square lower edge of barn block.

2. Square upper edge of prepared scrappy ground strata (fig. 27).

3. Stitch barn block to ground strata.

4. Stay stitch your completed block to protect the bias edges from stretching and the seams from coming apart (fig. 28).

Congratulations! You have now built all four blocks for your SEASONAL SAMPLER.

Fig. 26. Silos and right side sky stitched in place

Fig. 27. Preparing to add scrappy ground strata

Fig. 28. Cropped image of completed winter barn block

Assembling Your SEASONAL SAMPLER and Beyond

SEASONAL SAMPLER **shown larger on p. 42**

Before going any further, please read through these process steps to gain an overview of the general plan.

I encourage you to adapt your steps as needed to suit your free pieced blocks and your vision for YOUR SEASONAL SAMPLER.

❧ Square each of your four blocks but DO NOT TRIM.

❧ Lay out the four blocks in an arrangement that is pleasing to you.

> **Design note**
> I elected to use an oversize, off-center four patch arrangement with spring (block 1) and summer (block 2) on the top row and autumn (block 3) and winter (block 4) on the lower row.

Because I wanted to avoid rigid boundaries and preserve the wide open feel of the blocks, I did not add any kind of sashing.

❧ If necessary, add additional fabric(s) to the exterior edges of your blocks.

> **Design note**
> I enlarged the left side of the spring block adding 3 inches of scrappy ground fabrics and sky. If you need to add several inches of width, think about adding trees, silos, fences, and even a smaller barn building to fill in that area.

❧ Adjusting the horizon lines as needed, stitch block 1 to block 2 but DO NOT TRIM.

❖ Adjusting the horizon lines as needed, stitch block 3 to block 4 but DO NOT TRIM.

❖ Consider the relative size of each row's sky and ground areas. Experiment with the outside edges using yardage from your stash to simulate borders. Take your time and play with the possibilities. DO NOT TRIM TOO SOON!

❖ Once you have determined the vertical size for each row, trim and square the upper and lower edges. DO NOT TRIM the left and right edges yet.

❖ Aligning the center seam of each row as desired, stitch the lower edge of the top row to the upper edge of the lower row.

❖ Trim and square the right and left side edges as desired.

❖ If you do not plan to add borders, stay stitch the outer perimeter of your SEASONAL SAMPLER to protect the integrity of all exposed seam lines. I use a neutral thread and stitch slightly less than ¼" from the outer edges.

❖ If you do plan to add borders, take some time to consider the many options. I elected to add a 1½" inner border (finishing at 1") and a 4½" scrappy strata / piano key border (finishing at 4").

❖ Before adding your borders, consider fabrics for the back of your quilt.

❖ If you are planning to hang your SEASONAL SAMPLER, you will need to add a hanging sleeve. As you make these final design choices, consider

Design note

During the construction of the four blocks, I had set aside three very different types of yardage from my stash for possible use on the back. When it was time to make a final decision, none of them suited the quilt top. I found a one yard piece in my stash that was perfect – thankfully, I was able to order more of the same several-year-old fabric online.

whether you want to use the backing fabric to create your sleeve or whether you want to use a contrasting fabric.

❖ Consider which fabrics you might want to use for binding. The final decision can wait until your SEASONAL SAMPLER has been quilted, but it is a good idea to select possible fabrics and set them aside now.

❖ Once you have made your decisions about the borders, cut and stitch them in place.

Design note

After adding the inner border (sides first, then top and bottom), I added the four outer borders in a clockwise manner, using partial seams to finish the corners. I wanted the borders to encircle the quilt top to emphasize the cyclical progression from spring into summer into fall into winter into spring, etc.

❖ After pressing and squaring your quilt top, stay stitch the outer edges—especially if your border (like mine) involves a number of exposed seam ends.

Quilting Your Seasonal Sampler

Longarm quilter Chris Ballard with Iris, her Nolting 24" ProSeries Longarm machine
PHOTO: Sammie Ballard

Chris has a special gift for listening to each quilt and letting it tell her how it wants to be quilted. That sounds so simple—but after working with her for over ten years, it is NOT an easy process.

With each new quilt, she consistently finds a way to add details and textures that enhance without overwhelming the piecing, and all without marking the quilt.

Take time to think about the many quilting options for your SEASONAL SAMPLER, and if you are quilting by checkbook, be sure to share your ideas with your quilter and listen carefully to their suggestions.

Ideas for Future Projects

Here are just a few ideas for future barn building projects:

❖ Turn a series of free pieced barn blocks into a group of individual wall quilts

❖ Turn your free pieced barns into one-of-a-kind pillow covers

❖ Make one-of-a-kind tote bags

❖ Design and create a vertically-oriented barn quilt for a long narrow wall

❖ Design and create a horizontally-oriented free pieced barn wall hanging for a wide area that needs to be filled, like the empty space above a wall of windows

❖ Design and create a large single barn and use it as the focal block of a medallion style quilt

❖ Combine a large free pieced barn with free pieced letters to create a priceless baby quilt

❖ Consider honoring a barn or other historic building in your local area by creating a free pieced quilt to be used for preservation efforts or consider memorializing in fabric a family barn that may now exist only in fading photographs.

However you choose to use or display your free pieced barns, enjoy the process and have fun!

Gallery
The Secret Society of Barn Builders

The **Secret Society of Barn Builders** is the international group of quilt makers who agreed to "test" the process notes for this book by creating their own original free pieced barns. Their simultaneously unique yet universally appealing quilts are showcased in this book's external Gallery along with the stories behind their work.

Be sure to visit **Build-a-Barn: The Blog** for more on the Gallery: http://thefreepiecedbarnproject.blogspot.com

Charter Members of The SSOBB

- ❖ Hilda Bakke (New Mexico) who blogs at Hilda's Hideout http://hildashideout.blogspot.com
- ❖ Chris Ballard (Tennessee) who blogs at Quilting 4 U http://quilting4u.blogspot.com
- ❖ Heidi Burkhardt (Baden-Württemberg, Germany) who blogs at Libellenquilts - http://libellenquilts.blogspot.com
- ❖ Katherine French (Maine) who blogs at Q.U.I. (Quilted Under the Influence)—http://quiltedundertheinfluence.blogspot.com
- ❖ Cathy Labath (Iowa) who blogs at Sane, Crazy, Crumby Quilting http://saneandcrazy.blogspot.com
- ❖ Valerie Levy (Nova Scotia, Canada) who blogs at Purple Boots and Pigtails—http://purplebootsandpigtails.blogspot.com
- ❖ Cherie Moore (Illinois) who blogs at The Quilted Jonquil http://quiltedjonquil.com
- ❖ Belinda Noel (Texas) who blogs at Brown Dirt Cottage http://browndirtcottage.blogspot.com
- ❖ Glenda Parks (Louisiana) who blogs at Quilts and Dogs http://quiltswissy.blogspot.com
- ❖ Julie Post (Iowa) who blogs at joe tulips quilts http://joetulipsquilts.blogspot.com
- ❖ Nancy Stevens (Pennsylvania) who blogs at Blogging, Near Philadelphia—http://nancynearphiladelphia.blogspot.com
- ❖ Brenda Suderman (Manitoba, Canada) who blogs at Scraps and Strings http://scrapsandstrings.blogspot.com
- ❖ Lynne Tyler (New Hampshire) who blogs at The Patchery Menagerie http://patcherymenagerie.blogspot.com
- ❖ Debbie Voigt (North Carolina) who blogs at From the Strawberry Patch http://strawberrypatchquiltworks.com

Acknowledgments

Near Pleasantville, Tennessee not long after a heavy rain
PHOTO: Alan Sefton

I owe so much to so many, but a special mention goes to the following people:

Larry Sefton, my husband, my best friend, most loyal supporter, and in-house photography/technology expert,

Our son, **Alan Sefton**, the patient listener, project consultant, and proofreader,

Our son and daughter-in-law, **Eric** and **Lauren Sefton** for believing in this project and for sharing their joyful young dog, **Darcy** (my in-house editorial supervisor),

My very special friends, **Lynne Tyler** and **Chris Ballard** for absolutely everything,

Jeanne Lachance for her pivotal honesty and insight,

The **staff of American Quilter's Society** for their role in SEE ROCK CITY's journey, including **Elaine Brelsford**, for her 2013 voice mail asking if I would be interested in turning SEE ROCK CITY into a block of the month pattern for AQS. That voice mail was the spark that led to this book,

Austin Kleon for graciously giving permission to quote from his book *Steal Like An Artist – 10 Things Nobody Told You About Creativity*,

Janet Berlo, Ph.D. for graciously giving permission to quote from her book *Quilting Lessons – Notes from the Scrap Bag of a Writer and Quilter*,

Nancy McDonough, Executive Director for Davies Manor and Certified Quilt Appraiser for her enthusiastic support,

Tonya Ricucci for sharing her free pieced letters and so much more on her blog and for introducing me to the liberated work of Gwen Marston,

Chris and Sammie Ballard, **Lynn Carson Harris**, **Alan and Larry Sefton**, and **Lynne Tyler** for allowing me to include their photographs in this book,

My former law firm co-workers for their interest and encouragement, with a special thank you to **Dena Edelen** for sharing her proofreading expertise,

My blog readers, those who comment and those who lurk, for sharing every step of this journey,

All those who saw and enjoyed SEE ROCK CITY at one or more of the AQS shows. A special thanks goes to those who took the time to send a photo and/or note letting me know they had seen my quilt in person. It was such fun to read your reactions and impressions,

And finally, to the **extraordinary charter members of The Secret Society of Barn Builders** for testing early drafts of the SEASONAL SAMPLER's process notes, creating amazing quilts, and sharing their unwavering enthusiasm.

THANK YOU!

About the Author

Copper-domed silos just south of Memphis, Tennessee
PHOTO: Larry Sefton

Julie Sefton blogs at Me & My Quilts – Exploring the Possibilities, where she and her alter ego are known as Quiltdivajulie. Her blog profile describes things this way: "It is all about the journey. I love creating and making quilts. Colorfully liberated, authentic, eclectic, and in love with the process—that's me."

Julie inherited her love of quilts from the work of both grandmothers and at least one great-grandmother. After a lifetime of sewing and crafting, in 2004 Julie finally took a Beginning Machine Piecing class at her local quilt shop. Since then, she has created and finished over 275 quilts.

Julie and her husband Larry live near Memphis, Tennessee. When they are not in their respective studios (Larry is a wood artist), they enjoy vacationing at the John C. Campbell Folk School in North Carolina, and spending time with their family – Alan, Eric, Lauren, and Darcy (their grand-puppy).

Julie Sefton at the AQS QuiltWeek® Chattanooga, Tennessee, 2014 PHOTO: Larry Sefton

"Write the books you want to read."
Austin Kleon